MORE THAN COOKIES & PUNCH

Tina Houser

As God continues to place before us all the possibilities for a full and rewarding life, the challenge is to serve with a willing spirit and wring every ounce of joy out of each opportunity. As you do, may you see His hand at work around you, in you and through you. Reaching the world…one child at a time.

TINA!

Warner Press, Inc   Anderson, IN 46018
©2006 by Warner Press, Inc

Library of Congress Control Number: 2006926770

Design, Layout & Illustrations: Kevin Spear
Written by Tina Houser
Editor: Karen Rhodes
Food Photography: Mike Meadows
Printed in Singapore

THANKS!

… for your help

… your encouragement

… your ideas

… your brainstorming

… your support

… and your precious friendship!

There are some special people who help stir up the creative juices in me, who have discovered that God made each of them in His image—creative individuals.

Heidi, my assistant and right-hand when I need more than the two God gave me, is a gem of a friend. Thank you for your undying willingness to serve and learn about children's ministry.

To Heather, thank you for getting me stirred up to imagine when I think there's not another creative thought left. You are a constant reminder that God brings out the best in us and we're never too old to let Him make something new and exciting out of our lives.

I also want to thank the incredible children's ministry team at First Church of God, Kokomo, for helping me with input and actually making each and every snack in this book: Stacy Lawson, Jamie Smith, Melissa Kidwell and Tina Long. Others who helped me process ideas were Mona Carroll and McKenzi Fenn.

To my son, Jarad, I say thanks for always making me feel like the best mom in the world and that nothing is impossible. And to my husband, Ray, who watches me at the computer from the other room many nights—thank you for encouraging me to use the gifts God has given me. I love you!

All these people share my passion and excitement for reaching children for Jesus, and for that I am so grateful to my Heavenly Father. It is indeed a wonderful calling!

CONTENTS

NEW TESTAMENT

HOW TO USE THIS BOOK

The snack ideas in this book are written mainly as individual projects, but a few are more effective if done with a partner or as a group activity.

Sunday School

How many times have you heard one of your children in Sunday school ask, "What's for snack today?" or "When are we going to have a snack?" When children are asked what they would like more of in Sunday school, the reply is almost unanimous…they want more snacks! We have our children for such a short amount of time, and there is so much to teach them—why not give them what they are wanting and teach them at the same time? If the curriculum you use doesn't have a snack suggestion, check the story index or the scripture index in the back of this book and insert a snack that goes along with your lesson for the day. Integrate the *Whatcha Think?* questions and discussion as the children participate in making their own snack—a portion of class time that had no objective now becomes time with purpose and results. Give yourself more real learning time by incorporating Bible-based snacks in your lesson.

Family Devotions

Make one night a week a special time when the before-bedtime snack is one that the family makes together. Ask the children to look up the Bible verse where the story is found. *The Main Thing* is written at a third-grade level so children can read the story to the family. Children can take turns choosing which snack they will make. Also, some snacks (such as the Pizza Snake) can be used as a meal. When adults are asked what room of the house they remember with fondness, the kitchen is most often the answer. The smells and sounds of the kitchen are kept alive in family memories.

Home Schools

What a fun way to add practical lessons in measuring, reading, comprehension and following directions while encouraging cooperation and creativity. Use these snack activities in your home school lesson plans! Cookie cutters can be used to create special shapes in an otherwise boring sandwich to reinforce Bible lessons learned at home or church.

Service Projects

- Make extra snacks and take them to someone as a gift of appreciation.

- Prepare a snack that reinforces last week's Sunday school lesson and let your child take it to his or her teacher to show that the lesson really stuck.

- Take multiples of a snack to a retirement complex and encourage the children to tell about the snack's significance.

BODY BUILDING

God Created Man

Genesis 1:26—2:7

The Goodies

grape (or cherry)
little fruit snacks
pretzel sticks
cheese snack sticks

Gadgets & Gizmos

paper plate

The Main Thing

On the sixth day God said, "Let us make people in our image." God made a man's body from the dust on the ground and then breathed life into what He had made. God intended for man to be in charge of the rest of what He created. Man was supposed to take care of the animals, fish, birds, plants and everything else on earth. God also told people to have children so there would be more people. When God looked at what He had created, He smiled and thought it was good. On the seventh day God rested.

The Fun Stuff

Have the above ingredients available for the children to create a person. Make a person along with them to give them an idea of how to do it, but allow them freedom to create.

- A grape or cherry can be used as the head.

- Pretzels can be arms and legs.

- Cubes of cheese make the body.

- Little fruit snacks work as the hands and feet.

- Use the pretzel sticks to hold the pieces together.

PIZZA SNAKE

Adam and Eve Sin

Genesis 2:8—3:24

The Goodies

1 can of refrigerated pizza dough
pizza sauce
finely shredded mozzarella cheese
pepperoni slices
1 super-thin, long slice of carrot
1 black olive
1 T flour

Gadgets & Gizmos

cookie sheet
condiment squirt bottle
vegetable peeler
wax paper
paper plates
pizza cutter

The Main Thing

When God created the world He put Adam and Eve in a beautiful garden. God would come to Adam and Eve each day and talk with them. In the garden God put two special trees—one was the Tree of Life, and those who ate from it would live forever. The other was the Tree of the Knowledge of Good and Evil—those who ate from that tree would die. God told Adam and Eve they could eat anything in the garden, except from the Tree of the Knowledge of Good and Evil. One day a serpent came to Eve and told her it was alright for her to eat from that tree. She protested, but she finally ate from it; then she gave some to Adam. Immediately, they knew they had done wrong in God's sight. When God came to Adam and Eve that evening they were afraid to talk with Him because they had disobeyed. God punished them by sending them out of the beautiful garden, and He also told them, from that time on, there would be pain and sorrow in their lives.

The Fun Stuff

- Beforehand, preheat the oven according to the pizza dough package.
- Fill the squirt condiment bottle with pizza sauce.
- Roll the dough out on a surface that has been very lightly dusted with flour. Keep about an inch border on the dough that does not get toppings.
- Let the children layer pepperoni slices over the dough.
- In a zig-zag motion, squirt pizza sauce over the slices. (There should be a layer of ingredients between the dough and the sauce to prevent the dough from getting too soggy and not cooking properly.)

- Sprinkle mozzarella cheese over the pepperoni and sauce until you can't see those ingredients.
- Start on one of the long sides and roll the dough in jelly-roll fashion.
- When it is completely rolled, pinch the edge into the dough that it lays against. This will seal the roll. Round the ends as you seal them so they're not flat across.
- As you move the pizza dough roll to a cookie sheet, place it on the cookie sheet in an "S" shape with the seam side against the pan.
- Bake according to the pizza dough package (usually about 20 minutes) or until the dough is golden brown. This will make the body of the snake.
- After the snake is removed from the oven the face can be added by slicing one black olive in half for the eyes.
- Make a carrot curl for the tongue of the snake by slicing a very thin piece of carrot lengthwise. By the time you finish decorating the pizza snake's face it should be set enough to slice.

Whatcha Think?

- Everything was wonderful in the garden.
- Why do you think Eve listened to the snake?
- Why do you think Adam and Eve hid from God when He came to talk to them?
- Have you felt like hiding from your parents when you did something wrong?
- Do you ever feel like hiding from God?

This snack can also be used with:

The Brass Serpent
(Numbers 21:4-9)

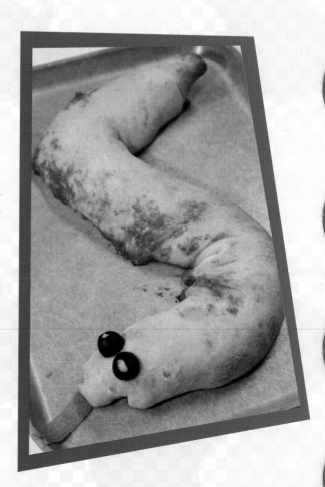

13

SLUSHY RAINBOW

God's Promise to Noah

Genesis 9:1-17

The Goodies

4 brightly colored sports drinks

Gadgets & Gizmos

ice cube trays
clear glasses
blender that will crush ice
straws
plastic spoons

The Main Thing

Once the waters from the flood went down, the animals came out of the ark, and Noah's family began to build their new home. To Noah, to all the people who would follow, and to all the creatures of the world, God made a new promise. He promised never to send another flood to kill all living creatures and destroy the earth. God gave Noah a new sign that would be a reminder of this promise—the rainbow. Even though clouds would come over the earth, there would also be a rainbow as a reminder of the promise God made.

The Fun Stuff

- Beforehand, fill the compartments of the ice cube trays halfway with the sports drink and freeze completely. (Depending on the amount of time you have, you may want to make the slushy mixtures right before your time with the children and place it in the freezer until you need it. Don't leave too long or you'll have a giant ice cube!)

- Let children help place one color of frozen sport drink in the blender.

- Add another cup of the sport drink of the same color and blend until the two turn to slush.

- Gently spoon about a one-inch layer of the slush mixture in the clear glass.

- Blend the ice cubes of the next color until it is slushy, and then pour a one-inch layer on top of the last color.

- Continue doing this until all the colors of frozen sport drinks are used. If your glasses are big enough and you have extra slushy of each color, you can make additional layers.

Whatcha Think?

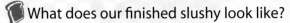 What does our finished slushy look like?

God gave us the rainbow as a reminder.

What is the rainbow supposed to remind us of?

How do you think Noah felt when God made this promise?

Why did God send the flood in the first place?

SHORTCAKE OR TALL CAKE

The Tower of Babel

Genesis 9:18—11:9

The Goodies

pound cake
strawberries
bananas
whipped topping

Gadgets & Gizmos

milk bottle cap
plastic spoons
baby spoon or ice cream sample spoon
large paper plate

The Main Thing

At one time in the Old Testament people thought it was possible to build a tower that would reach the sky. They worked together laying the bricks and they watched the tower rise higher and higher. What they were doing, though, did not please God. They were thinking so much about their precious tower they weren't thinking about God any longer. Soon they might forget about God altogether.

So God decided to do something to get their attention. Until then, everyone spoke the same language. But God was about to change that—He confused the language of the people so they no longer understood each other. They couldn't continue building the tower because they didn't know what the others were saying. Eventually those who spoke the same language found one another and moved away to live together in their cities.

The Fun Stuff

- Beforehand, slice the pound cake in very thin slices, no more than ¼". Using a very sharp knife will help get the slices thin.

- Also, slice the strawberries thin.

- Give the children a large plate to work on, when their tower falls you want it to land on a surface they can eat off of.

- Place sliced strawberries, bananas and the whipped topping where the children can reach them.

Give each child a slice of the pound cake and a bottle cap. Use the bottle cap as a cookie cutter and make a circle.

Encourage the children to start at an edge of the pound cake and cut other circles as close together as possible in order to have several circles for building their towers.

Start the tower by laying down one circle of pound cake on the plate.

Place a strawberry on top of that.

Use the baby spoon to dip out a very small amount of whipped topping for the next layer.

Place a thin slice of banana on top of the whipped topping.

Add another slice of pound cake and continue building. The order is cake, strawberry, topping, banana.

See how high you can make your tower before it topples.

Whatcha Think?

When you were concentrating on making your tower, were you able to do anything else?

When you're putting something together or building something you're interested in, it's difficult to think about other things. The people who were building the Tower of Babel were thinking about their tower so much they weren't spending time being with God.

How would you feel if all of a sudden your friends didn't understand what you were saying and they were speaking in a language you didn't know?

Why do you think some of the people moved away?

PRETZEL LADDER

Jacob's Dream

Genesis 27:42—29:12

The Goodies

2 large stick pretzels
5 small stick pretzels
canned squirt cheese

Gadgets & Gizmos

wax paper

The Main Thing

Jacob was traveling through the wilderness by himself. The sun was going down and Jacob found a rock to be his pillow for a night's sleep. While Jacob was asleep he dreamed he saw a ladder that went to heaven. Angels were going up and down the ladder.

Jacob dreamed that God spoke to him and said, "I will be with you wherever you go." God also told Jacob that some day he would return to the land he was sleeping on. God promised to give that land to Jacob and his descendants.

The Fun Stuff

 Let the children place the 2 large pretzel sticks parallel to one another, 2"-3" apart on a piece of waxed paper. These will make the sides of a ladder.

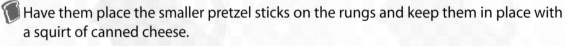 Have them place the smaller pretzel sticks on the rungs and keep them in place with a squirt of canned cheese.

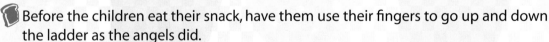 Before the children eat their snack, have them use their fingers to go up and down the ladder as the angels did.

Whatcha Think?

🍞 What do think was going through Jacob's mind when he woke up?

🍞 God promised to be with Jacob and God promises to be with us wherever we go.

FETTUCCINI STRIPES

Joseph's Coat of Many Colors

Genesis 37:1-4

The Goodies

small Jell-O™ packages (green and red)
uncooked fettuccini
parmesan cheese

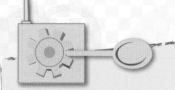

Gadgets & Gizmos

old pots
water
strainer
salt
poster board
Styrofoam plate
plastic knife
colander

The Main Thing

Jacob settled in the land of Canaan and raised his family. Joseph had been born to Rachel, Jacob's true love, when Jacob was very old. This caused Jacob to love Joseph more than his other sons. As a teenager Joseph tended his father's sheep. Occasionally, he would tell his father about bad things his brothers were doing. Joseph's brothers disliked him because of the special attention he got from their father. One day Jacob gave Joseph a beautiful robe as a gift. This made the brothers hate Joseph even more so that they could not find anything pleasant to say about their little brother.

The Fun Stuff

Beforehand:

Prepare both packages of Jell-O™ according to the instructions on the box.

Each package of Jell-O™ requires 4 cups of water.

Bring the water to a boil and add the Jell-O™, stirring until it is dissolved.

Add some of the fettuccini and boil according to pasta instructions. (Each child will need about 6 pieces of each color.)

Boil fettuccini (6 pieces) in green Jell-O™, 6 pieces in red Jell-O™ and 6 pieces in plain water.

Drain the fettuccini, keeping the colors separate.

If preparing the day before, store in an airtight container.

Also trace the coat template onto poster board and cut out.

If the children like, they can add Parmesan cheese to the coat before eating.

Have children lay the fettuccini on their plate alternating colors and keeping each piece of pasta up against the piece next to it. The plate should be covered with stripes of fettuccini tight against one another.

Lay the poster board cut-out of the coat on top of the linguini.

Cut around the template with a plastic knife and discard the excess.

What you have left is a beautiful coat of many colors for Joseph.

Whatcha Think?

- What do you think Joseph's coat looked like?

- Let's make a coat for Joseph that is stripes of many colors.

- Who do you think made the coat for Joseph?

- Why was the coat so special?

- Do you think you would have felt like the brothers if you had a sister or brother like Joseph?

- When the brothers saw Joseph wearing the coat what did it remind them of?

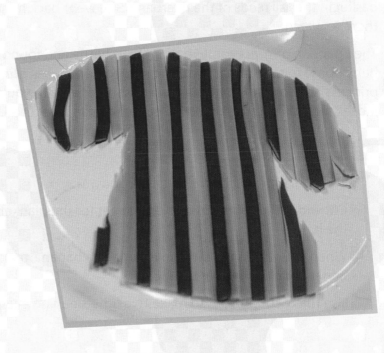

WAFFLE CONE BASKET

Baby Moses in the Bullrushes

Exodus 1:1—2:10

The Goodies

waffle cone cup
½ banana
sheet of fruit roll up
chocolate whipped topping
cake sprinkles

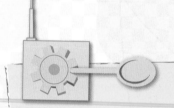

Gadgets & Gizmos

plastic knife

The Main Thing

There were many Israelites living in Egypt. Pharaoh became frightened that they would try to take over the country. But how could he stop them? He tried working them harder, but the harder they worked, the stronger they got.

Finally, he decided that every newborn baby boy would be thrown into the Nile River. A special baby boy was born at this time. For several months his mother was able to keep him hidden but soon he became too big to hide anymore. So the mother made a basket for a baby bed. She put him in the basket and took him to the edge of the river, where she carefully placed the basket in the tall reeds of the riverbank. She went back home, but left the baby's sister, Miriam, there to watch.

The Egyptian princess came to the Nile to bathe and found the basket. She decided to take the baby home to raise as her own. She named him Moses. Miriam, Moses' sister, approached the princess and told her that she knew of someone who would love to help her care for the baby. Moses' mother got to take care of her precious son after all.

The Fun Stuff

- Cut a banana in half for the baby's body.
- Cut wide strips of the fruit roll-up sheet for the blanket that will be wrapped around the baby.
- When you wrap the fruit strip around the banana, make sure you leave enough banana sticking out for the face.
- Use the cake sprinkles to make two little sleeping eyes.

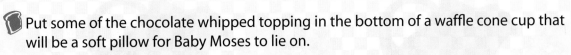

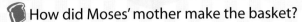
Put some of the chocolate whipped topping in the bottom of a waffle cone cup that will be a soft pillow for Baby Moses to lie on.

Then gently place the banana baby on the whipped topping.

Whatcha Think?

How did Moses' mother make the basket?

What else do you think she put inside the basket?

Why did Moses' mother leave Moses at the river's edge?

How do you think Miriam felt as she watched the basket?

SHEPHERD'S STAFF

Moses Becomes a Shepherd

Exodus 2:11-25

The Goodies

candy cane
1 c melting chocolate
1 t shortening
crushed candy bars
sprinkles
chopped nuts

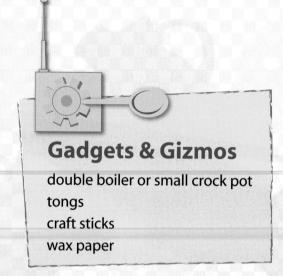

Gadgets & Gizmos

double boiler or small crock pot
tongs
craft sticks
wax paper

The Main Thing

Even though Moses had been raised in the palace of the Egyptian Pharaoh, he disliked the ways of the Egyptians. He knew he was an Israelite by birth and he wanted to follow the One True God. One day he saw an Egyptian beating an Israelite. Moses jumped in to help and killed the Egyptian. Hoping no one would find out, Moses hid the dead man in the sand. The next day Moses saw two Israelites fighting and he told them to stop. They had seen what Moses had done to the Egyptian the day before and that frightened Moses so he ran away. He stopped at a well where seven sisters came to water their sheep. When other shepherds tried to bully them, Moses helped the sisters. They took him home to their father, Jethro, and Moses worked for Jethro as a shepherd for many years. Moses also married one of Jethro's daughters.

The Fun Stuff

Melt the chocolate and the shortening at a very low temperature, either over a double boiler or in a small crock pot.

The crock pot will keep the chocolate melted consistently.

The chocolate can also be melted in a microwave, but do it in small time intervals, stirring between.

Let the children hold their candy cane with a pair of tongs at the very end of the candy.

Have them dip it into the pot of melted chocolate and then hold it over the pot while the excess drips off.

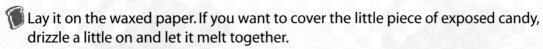 Lay it on the waxed paper. If you want to cover the little piece of exposed candy, drizzle a little on and let it melt together.

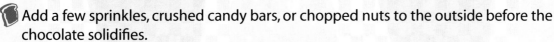 Add a few sprinkles, crushed candy bars, or chopped nuts to the outside before the chocolate solidifies.

Whatcha Think?

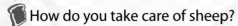 What does a shepherd need to know about sheep?

What do you take care of sheep?

What kind of special equipment does a shepherd need?
(He needs a staff that is a large walking stick with a crook on one end.)

What is the crook used for?
(If sheep get caught in some briars, the shepherd is able to help pull them out by putting the crook around the sheep.)

This activity can also be used with:

Samuel Anoints David
(1 Samuel 16:1-13)

The Shepherds and the Angels
(Luke 2:8-20)

A SNAKE...A ROD

God Gives Moses Three Signs

Exodus 4

The Goodies

¼ c margarine

cooking spray

6 c Rice Krispies™ cereal

chocolate candies

Fruit Loops™ cereal

1 pkg (10 oz) marshmallows =
40 large or 3 c miniature

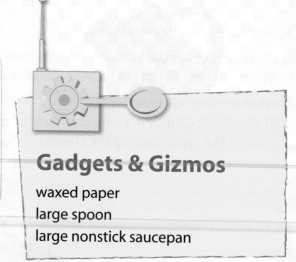

Gadgets & Gizmos

waxed paper

large spoon

large nonstick saucepan

The Main Thing

When God told Moses to go before Pharaoh and demand that he let the Israelite people go, Moses was afraid. Moses asked God for a sign that Pharaoh would believe. God asked Moses what he had in his hand—Moses said it was his rod. Then God told him to lay the rod down. When Moses did, the rod became a snake. This frightened Moses and he turned to run when God told him to pick it up by the tail. When Moses touched the tail of the snake, it turned back into his rod.

God gave Moses two other signs. He told Moses to stick his healthy hand into his cloak and pull it out. When his hand came out of his robe it was covered with sores. When he put it back in the robe the sores disappeared.

The third sign God gave Moses was to pour some water from the Nile River on the ground—when it hit the ground it would turn to blood. Moses was still hesitant about going to Pharaoh because he wasn't good at speaking, so God told him that He would send Aaron (Moses' brother) along with him to speak the words God instructed.

The Fun Stuff

Right before the children are ready to do this activity make a batch of Rice Krispie treats by following this recipe.

- Melt ¼ cup margarine in a large saucepan over low heat.

- Add 40 large or 3 cups miniature marshmallows and continue to stir until the marshmallows are completely melted.

- Remove them from the heat.

- Stir in 6 cups Rice Krispies™ until the cereal is coated with the melted marshmallow mixture.

The Rice Krispies Treats™ cool down very quickly, so you can almost immediately dish out portions for the children to work with.

- Give each child a piece of waxed paper.
- Spray the child's hands lightly with cooking spray so the Rice Krispies™ mixture will not cling to their hands as they work with it.
- Give each child about ¾ cup of the mixture to work with.

Say: *When Moses asked God for a sign to take to Pharaoh, God asked Moses what he had in his hand. What did Moses have in his hand? Let's make our Rice Krispies™ into the rod that Moses carried.*

- Have children form their Rice Krispies™ into a rod and lay it on the wax paper.

Say: *When God told Moses to lay the rod down on the ground, what happened to it? Let's turn our rod into a snake.*

- Have children reshape their Rice Krispies™ into a snake.
- Provide chocolate candies for eyes, and Fruit Loops™ to make a rattle on the tail of the snake.

Whatcha Think?

- When God told Moses to pick the snake up by the tail, what happened? Let's turn our snake back into a rod, and then eat it.
- How would you have reacted when the rod turned into a snake?
- How do you think that made Moses feel when he saw God's power in this sign?
- Even with this remarkable sign, Pharaoh would not let the people go. Sometimes God does marvelous things for us and we fail to recognize it or understand how He is trying to get our attention.

CHARIOT WHEELS

Crossing the Red Sea

Exodus 13:20—15:21

The Goodies

rice cakes
cheese slices
gumdrops

Gadgets & Gizmos

paper plates
plastic knife

The Main Thing

God sent many plagues upon Egypt to convince Pharaoh to let the Israelites leave the country. Finally, after the angel of death visited the homes of all the Egyptians and took their firstborn children, Pharaoh sent the Israelites away. They gathered their belongings quickly and left Egypt. God led the Israelites in a cloud during the day and a pillar of fire at night.

But Pharaoh changed his mind once again and sent his army with all the chariots of Egypt to bring back the Israelite slaves. The Israelites came to the Red Sea and didn't know how to get across it. They knew the chariots of Pharaoh's army were getting closer. God told Moses to raise his rod over the sea. When Moses did as God instructed, the waters of the sea separated and made it possible for the Israelites to cross. Close behind them was the Egyptian army. Moses dropped his rod and God made the waters of the sea fall in around the army. The Israelites were able to get away.

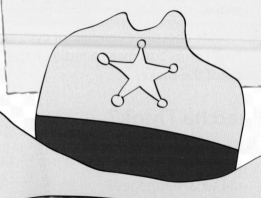

The Fun Stuff

- Have the children cut their cheese slice into strips about ¼" wide.
- Lay the strips across the rice cake, intersecting at the center. This will make the spokes of the wheel.
- Cut some of the cheese strips in short segments to outline the rice cake.
- Add a gumdrop at the center intersection to make the hub of the wheel.

Whatcha Think?

- What would you find a wheel on?
- In the story of Moses leading the people out of Egypt, is there anything that would have a wheel on it? Perhaps, the Israelites had wagons to carry their belongings.
- Pharaoh sent his army with all the chariots of Egypt to try to stop the Israelites. How many wheels are on a chariot?
- How many wheels do you think there were in the whole Egyptian army?

This story could also be used with:
Elijah and the Chariot of Fire (2 Kings 2)

MT. SINAI CONES

God Gives Moses the Ten Commandments

Exodus 19:1-25

The Goodies

ice cream sugar cones
canned white icing
green food coloring
minimarshmallows
shelled sunflower seeds

Gadgets & Gizmos

craft stick
paper plate

The Main Thing

Only a few months after leaving Egypt, the Israelites camped at the base of Mt. Sinai. Moses went up the mountain to talk with God. God told Moses He wanted the Israelite people to be His people and He expected them to obey Him.

Moses went down the mountain and talked to the people who agreed they wanted to do as God commanded. Moses then went back up the mountain to return the message to God. God appeared to the people in a thick cloud. The people were not allowed to touch the mountain, though. Many times Moses went up the mountain to speak with God and down the mountain bringing messages to the people. God instructed them to follow ten rules called the Ten Commandments so that they would live in obedience to Him.

The Fun Stuff

- Beforehand, blend thoroughly a can of white icing with several drops of green food coloring.

- Stand an ice cream sugar cone on a paper plate.

- With a craft stick, apply green icing all over the cone.

    Say: *We are going to change this ice cream cone into the mountain that Moses climbed to talk with God. Moses needed a path to walk on.*

- Make a path by applying a trail of sunflower seeds, winding up the mountainside.

    Say: *How did God appear to Moses? He was in a thick cloud. Clouds remind me of marshmallows.*

- Apply minimarshmallows around the top of the mountain.

Whatcha Think?

- Who was allowed to go up the mountain?
- What are commandments?
- Why is it important for us to follow God's commandments?

This snack activity can also be used with:

- The Temptations of Christ (Matthew 4:1-11; Mark 1:12-13; Luke 4:1-14)
- The Sermon on the Mount (Matthew 5—7; Luke 6:17-49)
- The Mount of Transfiguration (Matthew 17:1-13; Mark 9:2-13; Luke 9:28-36)
- Abraham Offers Isaac on Mt. Moriah (Genesis 22:1-19)

COMMANDMENT CRACKERS

The Ten Commandments

Exodus 20:1-17

The Goodies

club crackers
squirt cheese

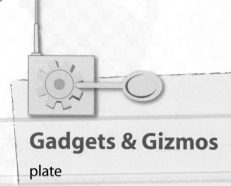

Gadgets & Gizmos

plate

The Main Thing

Moses brought the tablets with the Ten Commandments on them back to the people. God said to the Israelites:

1. Do not worship any gods except me.
2. Do not make idols.
3. Do not misuse the name of God.
4. Remember the Sabbath because it belongs to God.
5. Respect your father and mother.
6. Do not murder.
7. Be faithful to the person you married.
8. Do not steal.
9. Do not tell lies.
10. Do not want anything that belongs to someone else.

The Fun Stuff

- Give each child 5 club crackers.
- Tell them to write a number between 1 and 10 on each of the crackers using the squirt cheese. They can choose any 5 numbers they want; they do not have to be in order.
- Beforehand, write the numbers 1-10 on pieces of paper and put them in a container.
- Once the cheese numbers are on the crackers, draw out one of the numbers from the container.

If any of the children with that number can tell you what commandment belongs to that number, then everyone with that number on their cracker can eat it.

If no one can tell what commandment goes with that number put the piece of paper back in the container.

When other commandments are eliminated they may be able to come up with it the next time it is drawn.

Continue drawing numbers until all the cheese numbers have been called.

CLUSTER OF SWEET GRAPES

The Twelve Spies

Numbers 13—14

The Goodies

package sugar cookie dough
red and blue food coloring

Gadgets & Gizmos

sturdy cereal bowl (not Styrofoam)
spoon
aluminum foil
cookie sheet
cooking spray

The Main Thing

The Israelites were very, very close to the land of Canaan, the Promised Land. God told Moses to send twelve spies to spy on the land and find out what the land was like. Joshua and Caleb were among the twelve spies.

The spies were in the Promised Land for forty days and found beautiful fields of grain and wonderful vineyards. When the spies returned from their mission, they brought back some of the foods they found there to show everyone. It took two men to carry one cluster of grapes on a pole between them, because the fruit was so large. It was amazing! Caleb wanted to go at once to take the land, but ten of the spies didn't want to go. They reported seeing men in the land that were so big they made the spies look like grasshoppers. The people did not have faith in God. To punish them, God commanded them to go back out in the wilderness until everyone twenty years old or older had died.

The Fun Stuff

- Let the package of refrigerated cookie dough set out to soften.
- Put enough dough for 2-3 cookies into each child's bowl. Do not use disposable bowls because they are not sturdy enough for the vigorous mixing the children will do.
- The child will press the dough with the back of the spoon to soften. Create a small dip in the dough.
- Put 2 drops of blue and 4 drops of red food coloring into the dip.

🍞 Mash the food coloring into the dough until the color is even and the cookie dough has turned purple.

🍞 Lightly spray the child's hands before working with the dough. Roll little balls of dough about the size of a marble.

🍞 Arrange them on the piece of foil (or directly onto a cookie sheet) about ¾" apart and in the arrangement of a cluster of grapes.

🍞 Each portion should yield about 15 grapes to make the cluster. If the dough cluster is on a piece of foil, pull it onto a cookie sheet. Bake at 350° for 10 minutes. Each small ball of dough will spread to touch the others around it and will look like a grape cluster when it comes out of the oven. Allow the cookie 3-5 minutes to cool before removing it from the foil or cookie sheet.

Cut a stem from the brown construction paper and some leaves from the green paper to place at the top of the cluster of grapes. What a masterpiece!

Whatcha Think?

🍞 Make the expression that you might have had when you saw the huge grapes for the very first time.

🍞 How did the men carry the cluster of grapes?

🍞 Why were the Israelites afraid of going into the Promised Land?

🍞 Why was God displeased with the Israelites?

This snack activity can also be used with:

📖 The Parable of the Tenants
(Matthew 21:33-46;
Mark 12:1-12; Luke 20:9-19)

📖 Ahab Wants Naboth's Vineyard
(1 Kings 21)

SURPRISE ANGEL

A Donkey Speaks

Numbers 22:1-35

The Goodies

ice cream sugar cone
canned white icing
large marshmallow
yellow Lifesaver™
large twisted pretzel

Gadgets & Gizmos

plate
craft stick

The Main Thing

King Balak sent for the wise man of God, Balaam, for help. The large Israelite army was camped close by and King Balak was afraid they would attack. He knew if Balaam spoke against the Israelites they would become weak. Balaam did not want to go to King Balak, but God told him to go. God warned Balaam to speak only the words that he was given by God. Balaam got on his donkey and rode towards King Balak.

On the way, God sent an angel to stand in the road with a sword. Balaam did not see the angel, but the donkey did and ran into a field because she was afraid. Balaam beat the donkey for disobeying. Again, the angel appeared and the donkey crushed Balaam's leg against a stone wall. Balaam beat the donkey for disobeying. A third time the angel appeared and when the donkey saw it, the donkey lay down in the road. Balaam beat the donkey fiercely. God gave the donkey a voice and she asked Balaam, "Why are you doing that?" Then Balaam saw the angel who warned him one more time to speak only the words that God gave him.

The Fun Stuff

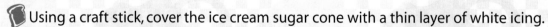

- Using a craft stick, cover the ice cream sugar cone with a thin layer of white icing.
- Push a large marshmallow onto the point of the cone for the head of the angel.
- Use icing to "stick" a large twisted pretzel to the cone to make the wings.
- Place a yellow Lifesaver™ on top of the marshmallow for the angel's halo.

Whatcha Think?

How do you think you would react if a donkey talked to you? Balaam didn't seem to notice.

Why do you think Balaam wasn't startled when the donkey spoke to him?

Why do you think God sent the angel to Balaam? God had already warned Balaam to speak only the words that he was given, but it must have been very important to God that Balaam follow His orders. It was so important God made a donkey speak!

This activity can also be used with:

The Angel Appears to Mary (Matthew 1:18-25, Luke 1:26-56)

Announcement of Jesus' Birth to the Shepherds (Luke 2:1-39)

Peter and John Released from Prison (Acts 5:12-42)

BRAIDED ROPE

Rahab's Red Cord

Joshua 1—2

The Goodies

red Twizzler™ rope licorice

The Main Thing

While Joshua was getting ready to lead the Israelites in a battle against Jericho, he sent two spies to check out the city. When the spies got inside the city, they talked with a woman whose house was on the city wall. Her name was Rahab. Someone sent word to the king that there were spies at Rahab's house, but when the soldiers came to search the house the spies could not be found. Rahab had hidden them in stalks of grain on the roof. Before the spies left Rahab's house she asked for their protection when the Israelites came to fight in Jericho. The men told her to hang a red cord from her window on the city wall and the Israelites would know not to harm her.

The Fun Stuff

🍞 Show the children how to lay the 3 pieces of the red Twizzler™ rope licorice on their plate and braid them to make a cord.

🍞 To make a more substantial cord, each string can actually be made up of 3 of the tiny strips of Twizzler™ licorice.

Whatcha Think?

🍞 Why was a red cord important in the story of Rahab and the spies?

🍞 Why do you think they chose a red cord instead of a brown cord?

🍞 Why do you think Rahab chose to help the spies?

CLOCK MUFFINS

Time Stands Still

Joshua 10—12

The Goodies

English muffin

12 raisins

2 stick pretzels

spreads (*peanut butter, flavored cream cheese, cheese spread, icing)

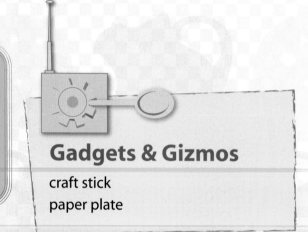

Gadgets & Gizmos

craft stick

paper plate

Special caution: If there are peanut allergies in your group, substitute the peanut butter with canned icing.

The Main Thing

The city of Gibeon had made peace with Joshua and the Israelites. But five enemy kings had gotten their armies together to go against Gibeon. Because the people of Gibeon were afraid of the armies, they called for Joshua and the Israelites to come help them. Joshua went to help them because God told him to go. God also told Joshua that they would have victory. The Israelites fought all day and the armies were scattering, but Joshua was afraid the enemy would come back the next day to fight. There was not enough daylight left to finish the fight. Because Joshua knew God was on their side, he looked up and told the sun and the moon to stand still. Time stood still. It was the longest day ever! The Israelites won the battle because God made time stand still.

The Fun Stuff

- Let children use a craft stick to put one of the spreads on their English muffin.
- Then place the 12 raisins where the numbers would be on a clock.
- Break the stick pretzels so they will be the right length for the hands of the clock.

Whatcha Think?

- You can't get your pretzel hands to move if they're in the spread. Time is standing still. What would it be like if it was always 12:00 noon? 3:00 in the afternoon? 7:00 in the evening? 11:00 at night?

- What could you do if it stayed light longer each day?

- What do you think the enemy did when they saw that the God of Joshua could make the sun and the moon stand still?

THE PROMISED LAND COOKIE

Dividing Up the Land

Joshua 13—19

The Goodies

roll of plain prepared cookie dough
canned white icing
green food coloring

Gadgets & Gizmos

deep cookie sheet
Styrofoam bowl
plastic spoon
large serving spatula
small disposable plates

The Main Thing

After Joshua led the Israelites into the Promised Land of Canaan, they had to fight the people living there to take possession. They had fought many battles and most of the Promised Land was theirs. Joshua was an old man and God gave him instructions on what to do next—divide the land between the twelve tribes of Israel and then let them finish conquering the people in their part of the land. Joshua did as God commanded. Some of the tribes went to the mountain country—others took the flat lands. God gave Joshua his own city because he had faithfully led the people.

The Fun Stuff

- Beforehand, press a roll of plain prepared cookie dough (no chips) onto a deep cookie sheet. Bake according to package instructions.

- Put a large spoonful of plain icing in the child's Styrofoam bowl.

- Drop 2, 3, or 4 drops of green food coloring onto the top of the icing for the child.

- Let the children stir the food coloring into their icing.

- When the food coloring and the icing are sufficiently mixed, each child will spread their icing onto the top of the sheet of cookie.

- Each child's icing will cover only a small portion of the cookie. Do not allow them to spread icing over the entire cookie.

Whatcha Think?

- The Promised Land was described as a land flowing with milk and honey.

- What do you think it looked like? After being in the desert, the green plants of the Promised Land must have looked wonderful to the Israelites! The green icing represents the beautiful things that grew in the Promised Land.

- The Bible tells us that the land was divided among the twelve tribes of Israel. Let's divide our Promised Land cookie.

- You will probably be able to tell the different areas of green that have been applied by each child, because the food coloring will vary slightly.

- Try to cut that area, making the cuts irregular because the land was not divided into squares, but according to special characteristics of the land.

- Dish out a piece for each child.

- This piece goes to the tribe of "Jennifer" (and so on). How do you think the people felt when they finally had a place to call home again?

CRUMBLING WALLS

Samson Brings Down the Walls

Judges 16:1-31

The Goodies

large box of Crispix™
1 stick of margarine
*¾ c peanut butter
1 lb powdered sugar
6 oz bag of chocolate chips

Gadgets & Gizmos

paper lunch sacks
scoop
large spoon
crock pot
paper plate
measuring cups

Special caution: If there are peanut allergies in your group, substitute the peanut butter with canned icing.

The Main Thing

The secret to Samson's strength was that God told him never to cut his hair. Samson revealed the secret to Delilah, who allowed the enemy to come in when Samson was asleep and cut his hair. In his weakened state, they were able to take him prisoner, put out his eyes and make him grind grain like an animal. During a big feast at the temple the rulers had Samson brought to them so they could watch him, blind and in his chains. They laughed and made fun of him! Samson asked a young boy to lead him to the pillars that supported the temple. There he prayed that God would give him strength one more time. Samson stood between the two main pillars of the temple and pushed against them as hard as he could. The stones of the temple tumbled down and everyone there was killed, including Samson.

The Fun Stuff

Right before class, put the chocolate chips, peanut butter, and margarine into the crock pot and turn it on the low setting, stirring the mixture as it melts.

Let the children pour the cereal into the crock pot where you will stir it until all the cereal is covered by the chocolate-peanut butter mixture.

Scoop a heaping cupful into each child's paper bag.

Have them pour about ⅓ c of powdered sugar into the bag.

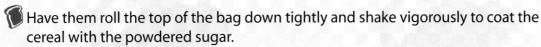 Have them roll the top of the bag down tightly and shake vigorously to coat the cereal with the powdered sugar.

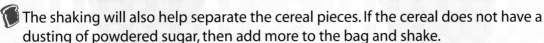 The shaking will also help separate the cereal pieces. If the cereal does not have a dusting of powdered sugar, then add more to the bag and shake.

Whatcha Think?

 What did Samson ask God to give him one more time?

Why do you think Samson wanted God's strength one more time?

What happened when Samson pushed on the pillars? The walls of the temple tumbled down. There was a terrible mess when the building collapsed.

Have children pour the contents of the bag onto the paper plate. This represents the stones of the temple that became a pile of rubble.

Another story this could be used for:
Joshua and the Walls of Jericho
(Joshua 5:13 – 6:27)

GRAIN GOODIES

Ruth Gleans Grain

Ruth 1:19—2:26

The Goodies

Rice Krispies™
apples
caramel dip

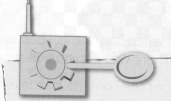

Gadgets & Gizmos

sharp knife
paper plates
plastic spoons

The Main Thing

Ruth and her mother-in-law, Naomi, returned to Naomi's homeland after their husbands had died. Ruth was determined to support herself and Naomi. She went to the grain field of a rich man named Boaz to glean what grain was left on the ground. Ruth picked up the grain, piece by piece, to take home so they could make bread to eat. Boaz admired Ruth because she was a beautiful woman and she worked without stopping. He also admired her because she was taking care of her mother-in-law. Boaz instructed his helpers to leave extra grain for Ruth. When Ruth returned home to Naomi, Naomi was amazed at the amount of grain Ruth was able to find.

The Fun Stuff

 Peel the apple and then slice it in very thin pieces.

Allow the children to cover their plate with the slices of apple.

Warm the caramel dip slightly by placing it in the microwave for a few seconds.

Have the children spoon out the caramel dip and spread it over the top of the apples.

Ask: *This is the ground. What was on the ground that Ruth picked up? What does "glean" mean?*

Sprinkle some of the rice cereal over the top of the caramel.

Whatcha Think?

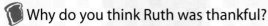 These are the grains of wheat that Ruth gleaned. Can you imagine picking up enough of these little pieces to make a loaf of bread!

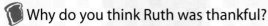 Why do you think Ruth was thankful?

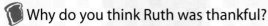 Why was Boaz so kind to Ruth?

Say: *Your food was much easier to get than Ruth's food, wasn't it?*

CHOCOLATE ANOINTING

Samuel Anoints David

1 Samuel 16:1-13

The Goodies

vanilla ice cream

chocolate syrup

assorted round candies

crumbles

small fruits (like maraschino cherries, blueberries)

Gadgets & Gizmos

bowl

spoon

The Main Thing

God sent Samuel to Bethlehem to anoint the person He had chosen to be the next king of Israel. The Lord told Samuel the new king would be one of Jesse's sons, but which one? Samuel filled his horn with oil and went to the feast that Jesse and seven of his sons would attend. Samuel looked at Jesse's oldest son and thought maybe he was the one because the young man was tall and handsome. But God told Samuel he wasn't the one.

As each of the seven sons of Jesse passed before Samuel, God told him that they were not the ones. Samuel was confused and asked Jesse if he had any other sons. The youngest boy was tending the sheep. Samuel sent for the boy whose name was David. As soon as Samuel saw David he knew this was the one God had chosen to be king. Samuel pulled out his horn of oil and anointed the boy by pouring oil on his head. David knew this was the sign that he would be the next king.

The Fun Stuff

Put a round scoop of ice cream in the bowl as the starting point of creating a head.

Have the children add crumbled candy bar or cookies to one side of the scoop to make the hair.

Then have them add small candies, cereal, or pieces of fruit to create a face.

Whatcha Think?

Now you have a face for the shepherd boy, David.

What happened when David came in front of Samuel?

🍞 What does it mean to anoint?

🍞 When Samuel anointed David, what did it symbolize? Anointing was a way of symbolizing that God had chosen this person and would be with the person. The oil that was poured on David would have run down over his head.

🍞 Let children pour chocolate sauce over their ice cream heads.

Say: *This ice cream has also been chosen for a special purpose!*

POUCH OF STONES

David Slays Goliath

1 Samuel 17:1-54

The Goodies

small pita pocket bread
¼ c raw ground hamburger
condiments
cooking spray

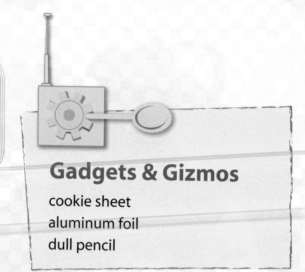

Gadgets & Gizmos

cookie sheet
aluminum foil
dull pencil

The Main Thing

David, the youngest son of Jesse, was sent by his father to check on his brothers as they faced the Philistines in battle. While David was at the army's camp, the giant Philistine, Goliath, appeared to make fun of the Israelites. David volunteered to represent the Israelite army in a face-off with Goliath. In preparation, the young shepherd boy picked up five smooth stones and placed them in his pouch. He then claimed the might of the One True God when Goliath laughed at the young opponent who came out to fight him. David reached into his pouch and pulled out one small stone. He placed it in his slingshot and whirled it at Goliath. The stone hit its mark on Goliath's forehead and brought the giant to the ground. God used an unlikely teenager to show His power.

The Fun Stuff

- Beforehand, preheat the oven to 375°. Cover a baking sheet with aluminum foil and spray it lightly with cooking spray.

- Have each child take ¼ cup of raw hamburger and make 5 little meatballs out of it.

- Use a dull pencil to mark areas in the foil so the children will not get their meatballs confused. You can even scratch their names into the foil.

- When everyone has made their meatballs, place them in the preheated oven for about 12 minutes. (Bake, rather than fry, to prevent hot grease splattering on the children.)

- When the meatballs are done, remove each child's and place them on individual paper towels.

- Give each child half of a pita pocket. They should be able to pull the sides of the pita apart to make the pocket.

Say: *This is the pouch that David carried. David went to a stream and picked something up. What did David pick up? Where did David put the stones?*

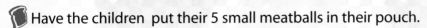 Have the children put their 5 small meatballs in their pouch.

Place a piece of masking tape on the wall about 9 feet from the ground.

Whatcha Think?

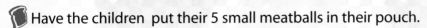 Imagine someone as tall as this mark is on the wall.

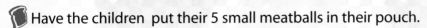 Imagine trying to fight against someone who was that big!

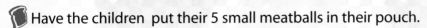 Do you think David was scared?

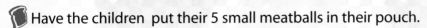 Why do you think God chose a shepherd boy to fight against someone as big as Goliath? David was glad to be used by God. God's power and might were shown because David made himself available to God.

DONUT ALTAR

Elijah and the Prophets of Baal

1 Kings 18:17-40

The Goodies

4 or 5 donut holes
blue drink

Gadgets & Gizmos

custard cup
soup bowl
small cup
straw

The Main Thing

Elijah challenged the prophets of Baal to prove their god was real by building an altar and asking their god to set fire to their offering. The prophets accepted the challenge but could not get their god to ignite the offering. Elijah doused the offering he was making to the One True God with 12 barrels of water. When he prayed and recognized God's authority in front of everyone, God sent down fire from heaven and burned up the offering. The fire even licked up the water that was in the trench surrounding the offering. The people were amazed at what they saw, and they believed in the God that Elijah worshipped.

The Fun Stuff

Have the children place a custard cup in the middle of a bowl.

Say: *Elijah built the altar with 12 stones. We can't get 12 donut holes in our custard cup, but we can build a mound to represent the altar that Elijah built.*

Have children build an altar by piling donut holes in the custard cup.

Say: *Before Elijah prayed for God to take the sacrifice, he poured water over the altar. Why do you think he poured water on the altar? Wouldn't it be impossible for it to catch fire if it was wet?*

Pour a small cup of blue drink in the bowl around the custard cup, which is like the trench around the altar. (Do not pour the blue drink over the donut holes, though.)

Say: *God sent down fire to burn up the sacrifice. The fire even lapped up the water that had flowed down into the trench around the altar.*

Tell the kids to use a straw to sip the blue drink from their bowl.

Say: *What do you think the people watching thought of God now?*

WONTON BUNDLES

Jacob's Family Moves to Egypt

Genesis 45:25—46:27

The Goodies

small pieces of fruit
wonton sheets

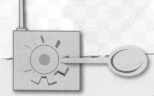

Gadgets & Gizmos

deep fryer
paper towel
scissors
slotted spoon
string

Whatcha Think?

Ask:

- What do you think Jacob packed to take to Egypt?
- What do you think the children did to help get ready for the move?
- Have you ever had to move? What was it like?

Say:

- Joseph's family didn't have suitcases so they bundled things in bags made of skin and tied ropes around them. The skins would keep the sand and any moisture from getting into the belongings.
- Let's do some packing of our own by making a bundle from a wonton and some fruit.

The Fun Stuff

- Cut a piece of string about 6" long
- Each child will lay their wonton out flat.
- Choose a piece of fruit, like pineapple, and dab it on the paper towel to get the extra juice off of it.
- Place the fruit in the center of the wonton. Pull the sides of the wonton up around the fruit, pinching the wonton together around the fruit.
- Use the string to tie around the wonton to secure the fruit bundle.
- An adult will drop the bundle in the deep fryer with a slotted spoon. It should only take about 15 seconds if the fryer is preheated. Set the bundle on a paper towel to drain grease from it. Remind the children that the string on the bundle is not edible and they need to clip it off.

The bundles will be cool enough to eat in one minute.

 Suggested fruit in small pieces: apples, cherries, pineapple, pears.

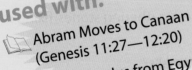 **This activity can also be used with:**

Abram Moves to Canaan
(Genesis 11:27—12:20)

Israel's Exodus from Egypt
(Exodus 12:31—42)

BRICK WALL
Nehemiah Rebuilds the Walls of Jerusalem
Nehemiah 2:19—6:19

The Goodies

graham cracker

peanut butter

Hershey's™ chocolate bar

Special caution: If there are peanut allergies in your group, substitute the peanut butter with canned icing.

The Main Thing

God sent Nehemiah to Jerusalem to help rebuild the walls. Before beginning, the rubbish had to be cleared. Some of the workers gathered the huge stones that would be put in place, others fixed meals for the workers and others stood guard so that the enemy would not try to destroy the work that was being done.

The Fun Stuff

- Have children use a wooden craft stick to spread a thin layer of peanut butter on one side of the graham cracker.
- Then, break apart the rectangular pieces of the chocolate bar.
- Push them into the peanut butter in rows with space in between to simulate mortar. It will look like a wall of bricks when finished.

Whatcha Think?

- Of all the jobs to be done, which would you choose—gathering stones, fixing meals or standing guard?
- Why do you think Nehemiah wanted to rebuild the walls?

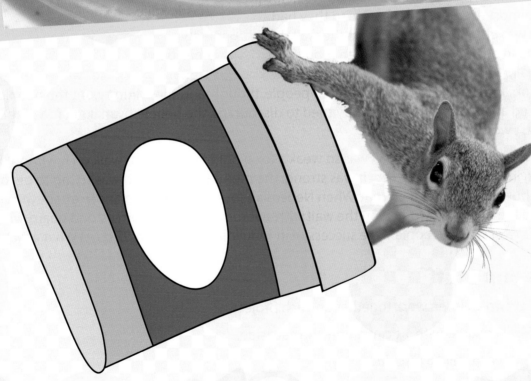

Other stories this snack can be used with:
Joshua and the Walls of Jericho (Joshua 5:13—6:27)

BISCUIT STONES FOR A WALL

Rebuilding the Walls of Jerusalem

Nehemiah 2:17—6:19

The Goodies

6 cans small biscuits
melted margarine
1 t cinnamon
¼ c sugar

The Main Thing

Nehemiah went to Jerusalem to help the people rebuild the city. Everyone was anxious to help… well, almost everyone. The first thing they had to do was pick up the rubble from the wall that had been destroyed. As they began rebuilding the wall, everyone had a job to do. Sanballat and Tobiah were enemies of the Jewish people, though, and they didn't want the people to succeed at rebuilding the wall. They tried to discourage the people by making fun of them but it didn't work.

The two men claimed the wall was so weak a fox wouldn't be able to walk on it without it falling in. But the people knew it was strong. The men said Nehemiah was trying to become ruler, but Nehemiah denied that. When Nehemiah found out about plans to attack the city, he armed the men who worked on the wall with swords and spears. Some stood guard while the others worked. The people were successful in rebuilding the wall in 52 days! What a victory!

Gadgets & Gizmos

foil mini-loaf pan
plastic knife
plate
small bowl

The Fun Stuff

- Let two children work together on each project.
- Mix ¼ c sugar with 1 t cinnamon and set aside.
- Give each child 6 biscuits.
- Have them cut across the biscuits to make 4 equal pieces from each biscuit.
- Roll each piece gently for just a second, enough to remove the points.
- Dip the small dough ball in some melted margarine, then roll it in the cinnamon/sugar mixture.
- Place the dough ball in the mini-loaf pan.

    Say: This is the first stone of rebuilding the wall of Jerusalem.

- Let the kids continue making "stone" pieces of the wall and placing them in the pan—rebuilding the wall.

Try to end with the dough balls even across the top.

Bake at 350° for 15 minutes.

Remove the loaf from the oven and run a knife around the edge to loosen it from the pan.

An adult should turn the pan upside down onto a plate to release the entire loaf; be careful of the steam being released.

Whatcha Think?

What different jobs do you think the people did to help build the wall?

Why didn't the people let Sanballat and Tobiah bother them?

Why do you think the people were willing to help rebuild the wall?

How did the wall get built so quickly? (everyone worked together)

How do we work together at our church to accomplish something for God?

This activity can also be used with:

The Temple Is Finished (Ezra 5—6 and Haggai 1—2)

MARSHMALLOW JIGGLER CROWNS

Queen Esther

Esther 1—7

The Goodies

1 pkg (8-oz) Jell-O™
1 c warm water
3 c miniature marshmallows or 12 large
cooking spray
various small colorful candies

Gadgets & Gizmos

13" x 9" pan
microwavable bowl
plastic knife
plate
wax paper

The Main Thing

The king of Persia was giving a big party and told his queen to come to the party, but she said no. This made the king angry so he decided to get a new queen.

Mordecai was a Jewish man who worked for the king. He brought his cousin, Esther, to the palace to be among the women from whom the king would choose a queen. Esther was beautiful and she loved God—the king chose her.

There was an evil man named Haman who didn't like the Jewish people. Haman convinced the king to make a law that all Jewish people would be killed. The king did not know that Mordecai and Esther were Jewish. Esther sent word for the people to pray for her. Then she gave a dinner for the king. When the king offered to give her anything she wanted, she asked that her people not be killed. "Who would do such a thing?" the king asked. It was Haman. The king was angry with Haman and his evil plan. Instead of killing the Jewish people the king sent Haman to his death.

The Fun Stuff

Beforehand, make the marshmallow Jell-O™ sheet by following these steps. Lightly grease a 13" x 9" pan with cooking spray.

Stir the gelatin and water in a bowl and microwave on high for 2½ minutes; gelatin should be dissolved.

Add the marshmallows, stir, and microwave on high for 2 minutes or until the marshmallows are partially melted.

Stir slowly until the marshmallows are completely melted, then pour the mixture into the 13" x 9" pan.

Refrigerate for at least one hour.

At class time:

Lightly spray each child's piece of wax paper with cooking spray.

Cut the marshmallow Jell-O™ sheet into rectangles 3" x 4" and give each child one of these.

Do not flip it over when moving it to the wax paper.

Let the children use a plastic knife to cut small triangles out of one of the longer sides. The triangles can be set aside to eat later. What will be left is a piece that looks like a crown.

Have the kids decorate the crown with jewels of various small candies.

Whatcha Think?

This is Queen Esther's crown. When do you think she wore her crown—all the time or for special things?

What do you like most about Queen Esther?

Why do you think Esther asked the people to pray for her before she went to see the king?

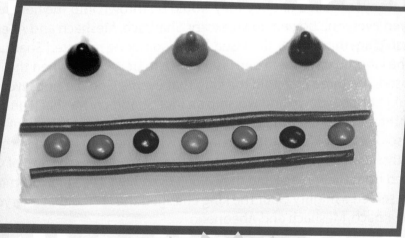

This activity can also be used with:

Saul Becomes King (1 Samuel 10:17-27)

David Becomes King of Israel (2 Samuel 5:1-4)

Solomon Becomes King (1 Kings 2:1-10)

THE FOURTH MARSHMALLOW

In the Fiery Furnace

Daniel 3

The Goodies

whole graham crackers
4 large marshmallows

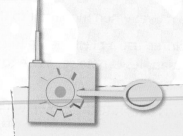

Gadgets & Gizmos

cookie sheet
oven

The Main Thing

King Nebuchadnezzar had a 90-foot-tall gold statue made for the people to worship. The law was made that when the music played everyone would have to bow down and worship the idol. If anyone failed to obey, they would be thrown into the fiery furnace. When the music played everyone bowed down except Shadrach, Meshach and Abednego. They refused to worship anything other than God. When someone reported Shadrach, Meshach and Abednego to the king, he gave them one last chance to bow down when the music played, but still they refused. The three men told the king that even if God did not save them from the furnace, they would not bow down and worship an idol. Shadrach, Meshach and Abednego were tied up and thrown into the furnace. The furnace was so hot that the flames jumped out and killed the soldiers who threw the men in. But, when the king looked in the furnace, he saw four men, not three, walking around, and one of them looked like the Son of God. The king had the men pulled from the furnace and they didn't even have the smell of smoke in their clothes! Surely, they served a mighty God! The king changed the law so that everyone had to worship the God of Shadrach, Meshach and Abednego.

The Fun Stuff

- Have each child place a whole graham cracker on the cookie sheet.
- Have children place one marshmallow on the graham cracker and identify it as Shadrach.
- Have them put the second marshmallow on the graham cracker and call it Meshach.
- As they add the third marshmallow tell them it is Abednego. Carry the cookie sheet to the oven, preheated to 350°, and place it inside.
- Now, tell the children to go wash their hands while all of you wait for the marshmallows to cook.

As soon as the children leave, add a marshmallow to each of the graham crackers.

 When the children return, they will look inside the oven door and count the marshmallows on their graham cracker. Now there are four!

Whatcha Think?

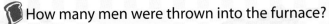 What did Shadrach, Meshach and Abednego do that angered the king?

How many men were thrown into the furnace?

What surprised King Nebuchadnezzar when he looked into the furnace?

Why were Shadrach, Meshach and Abednego not afraid?

We sometimes want God to rescue us, but even if he doesn't change our situation, we can know that God will be with us. We need to follow God even when our situations don't change.

CREATIVE WRITING

The Handwriting on the Wall

Daniel 5

The Goodies

pudding cup

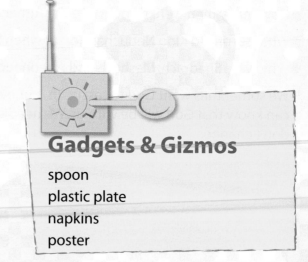

Gadgets & Gizmos

spoon

plastic plate

napkins

poster

The Main Thing

Belshazzar, the king of Babylon, worshiped idols and dishonored God. One day he gave a huge party and sent for the gold goblets from God's temple to be used at the party. As they were laughing and drinking, Belshazzar froze in fear. He saw the fingers of a man writing on the wall of the room, but there was no man, only the fingers. When he sent for the wise men to tell him what it meant, they had no idea. Then someone suggested asking Daniel to look at the words. Daniel told the king that the words were *Mene, Mene, Tekel, Upharsin* and they meant that God was going to give the kingdom to someone else. Ha! The king didn't believe it. That night, though, the enemy attacked and Babylon was captured—Belshazzar was no longer king.

The Fun Stuff

- Write *Mene, Mene, Tekel, Upharsin* on a poster to hang where all the children can read it easily.

- Give each child a pudding cup and a spoon. (Any flavor can be used as long as it is not multiple flavors that are layered.)

- Have the children empty the contents of the cup onto the plastic plate and spread it around as evenly as possible.

- Then let them pretend this is the wall in the party room and their fingers are writing the words from God.

- Ask kids to look at the poster and copy the words into their pudding. This is one time when licking fingers is perfectly fine!

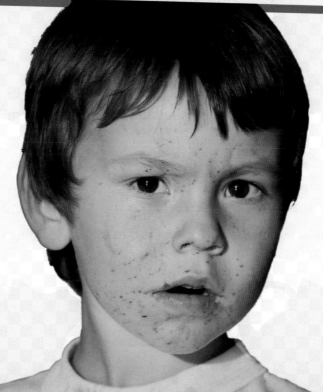

Whatcha Think?

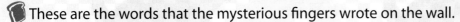 These are the words that the mysterious fingers wrote on the wall.

Whose fingers do you think they were?

Why do you think the fingers scared everyone so much?

What did the words mean?

A CHEESE-Y LION

Daniel in the Lions' Den

Daniel 6

The Goodies

bologna
small pretzel sticks
finely shredded cheddar cheese
raisins
carrot

Gadgets & Gizmos

plate
vegetable peeler

The Main Thing

Because Daniel was so wise and followed God, King Nebuchadnezzar made him one of the three most important men in his kingdom. Some people were very jealous of Daniel and wanted to get rid of him. They came up with a plan and convinced the king to make a law that no one could pray to any god, except the king. The men watched Daniel closely, and sure enough, they saw him pray—not once, not twice, but three times a day to the One True God. They hurried to report Daniel to the king, who had Daniel thrown in the lions' den.

The king was greatly troubled, but God caused the mouths of the lions to be locked shut, and they did not touch Daniel the entire time he was in the den. The next morning when the king went to the lions' den he found that Daniel was fine. The God Daniel worshiped had been faithful. Then the king had the men who had plotted against Daniel thrown into the same den of lions.

The Fun Stuff

🍞 Have kids make a lion using bologna as the head.

🍞 Sprinkle the finely shredded cheese around the edge of the bologna to make the mane.

🍞 Add raisins for eyes and a nose. Use pretzel sticks for whiskers.

🍞 For the mouth, make a long stroke with a vegetable peeler on the carrot—make two of these and place the ends together, starting at the raisin nose and coming down.

🍞 Separate the carrot peels in opposite directions to make the mouth. If they are too long cut them to the right length.

Say: *Does your lion have a scary face or a friendly face?*

Whatcha Think?

- What are lions like?
- What do they like to eat?
- How do you think Daniel felt when he found out it was against the law for him to pray to God?
- What do you think Daniel did while he was in the den with the lions?

TORTILLA WRAP

The Baby Jesus

Luke 2:1-39

The Goodies

small flour tortilla
½ hot dog
shoestring potato sticks

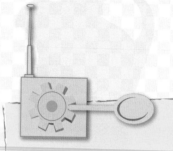

Gadgets & Gizmos

plastic knife
small paper plate

The Main Thing

Joseph and Mary had to travel to Bethlehem—King Herod wanted all the people to be counted. It was a difficult trip because Mary was about to have a baby. The city was crowded and the couple could find only a stable to rest in for the night. That night the baby was born, right there among the animals. Mary wrapped him in cloths to keep him warm and then laid him in the most comfortable place she could find, a manger filled with hay.

Outside of town there were some shepherds taking care of their sheep. Suddenly the dark sky became bright as an angel told the shepherds of the baby's birth. Other angels joined the first in praising the baby who was the Savior God had promised. The shepherds left their sheep and went into Bethlehem to find the baby. When they found Him, they bowed down and worshiped Him. Mary watched everything and her heart smiled because she knew she would remember this night for a very long time.

The Fun Stuff

 Beforehand, cut the hot dogs in half and warm them.

 Let the children use plastic knives to cut the tortilla into strips.

 Wrap the strips of tortilla around the half hot dog, criss-crossing the strips, but leaving the end of the hot dog sticking out.

Say: *Mary wrapped the baby Jesus in swaddling cloths so only his little face was sticking out. Let's pretend this wrapped hot dog is Baby Jesus.*

 Have the children place potato sticks on their plate and then lay the hot dog on top of them.

Whatcha Think?

🍞 Mary laid Baby Jesus in a manger filled with hay. Our potato sticks can remind us of the hay in the manger.

🍞 Why would there be hay in the manger?

🍞 Where do you think Mary got the cloths she wrapped Jesus in?

🍞 If you had been one of the shepherds, what do you think you would have done when you saw the angels?

🍞 What would you have done when you found the baby just like the angels said?

FRUIT BOAT

Fishermen Follow Jesus

Matthew 4:18-22

The Goodies

peach half
fruit roll-up sheet
fish crackers

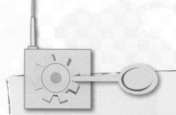

Gadgets & Gizmos

4"-5" piece of wooden skewer
paper plate
plastic knife

The Main Thing

One day when Jesus was just beginning His ministry, He was walking along the shore and noticed two brothers, Simon and Andrew, in their boat. Fishing was their business and they were taking care of the boat. Jesus said to the men, "Follow me and I will make you fishers of men." Simon and Andrew left their boat and followed Jesus. As they walked down the shore together, Jesus saw two more brothers, James and John, who were also fishermen. They were mending their fishing nets when Jesus said the same thing to them, "Follow me and I will make you fishers of men." They left their fishing business and followed Jesus. These four men would follow Jesus everywhere He went and would learn from Jesus as His disciples.

The Fun Stuff

- Have the children cut the fruit roll-up square at a diagonal to make two triangles (one triangle will make the boat's sail).
- Poke the skewer into the fruit triangle at one corner, then weave it in and out all the way down one side (about 3 times).
- Let children place their peach half on the plate and stick the end of the skewer into the center of the peach.
- Lay some fish crackers around the base.

Whatcha Think?

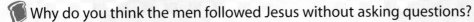 Why do you think the men followed Jesus without asking questions?

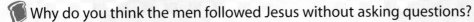 Do you think they ever missed their fishing business?

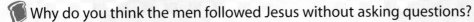 What did Jesus mean when He said they would "fish for men"?

WEDDING COOKIES

Jesus' Miracle at a Wedding

John 2:1-11

The Goodies

glazed donut holes
powdered sugar

Gadgets & Gizmos

Zip-lock sandwich bags

The Main Thing

Jesus, His mother Mary, the disciples and many other people had been invited to a huge wedding celebration. The party was still going on but there was no more wine to drink. When Mary found out she called Jesus aside and asked Him to do something. She then called several servants and told them to do whatever Jesus told them to do. Jesus instructed them to fill six huge jars with water, then pour out a glass and take it to the head of the party. When the man tasted from the glass, he was surprised that the best wine had been saved until the end of the party. Turning the water into wine was the first of the miracles Jesus performed.

The Fun Stuff

- Have kids put some white powdered sugar in a zip-lock bag.
- Ask them to put a glazed donut hole in the bag.
- Close the bag securely and shake the donut hole around in the powdered sugar until it is completely covered.
- Have kids make enough to eat some in class and to take home.
- Tell them, "Each time you eat them remember Jesus' first miracle. Or, share them with your family and tell them the story as you munch on them."

Whatcha Think?

- What special event was going on in this story?
- Have you been to a wedding?
- What did you see happening at the wedding?

There are all kinds of traditions that people add to their wedding ceremonies. It is a tradition in Mexico to make little round cookies rolled in white powdered sugar, wrap the cookies in white tissue paper, fringe the tissue paper, and then give them to all the guests to take home.

 Let's make something that looks like the Mexican Wedding Cookie.

This snack activity can also be used with:

Jacob Is Tricked by Laban (Genesis 29:13—31:55)

If you would like to make actual Mexican wedding cookies, the recipe follows:

The Goodies

2 c flour
½ t almond extract
½ t salt
1 c butter (unsalted)
2 t vanilla
¾ c finely chopped pecans
box of powdered sugar

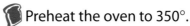 Preheat the oven to 350°.

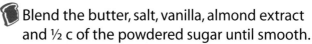 Blend the butter, salt, vanilla, almond extract and ½ c of the powdered sugar until smooth.

 Add the pecans and flour.

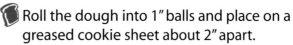 Roll the dough into 1" balls and place on a greased cookie sheet about 2" apart.

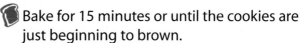 Bake for 15 minutes or until the cookies are just beginning to brown.

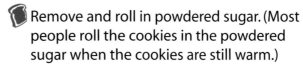 Remove and roll in powdered sugar. (Most people roll the cookies in the powdered sugar when the cookies are still warm.)

MAKE-YOU-GROW SHAKE

Jesus Grew

Luke 2:40-52

The Goodies

2 c skim milk

1 c frozen strawberries

¾ c frozen blueberries

½ banana

4 Equal™ sweetener packets

1 c ice cubes (about 7)

2 small containers strawberry/banana yogurt

Gadgets & Gizmos

blender

cups

The Main Thing

When Jesus was 12 years old He got to travel with His parents to the temple in Jerusalem for the Passover festival. They traveled with a lot of friends and relatives from Nazareth. On their return home Mary and Joseph did not realize that Jesus was missing from the group. When they noticed He was gone, they immediately returned to Jerusalem to find Him. They found Jesus sitting with the temple teachers, discussing deep questions and amazing them with His insight. When Mary told Jesus how frantic they were, He replied that He was merely doing His Father's business. Mary and Joseph took Jesus and returned to Nazareth where Jesus became wiser and learned many things. He grew physically as He got taller and stronger. He grew socially, learning how to get along with the people around Him. And He grew spiritually as He loved and served God.

The Fun Stuff

- An adult will need to work the blender, but give the children ingredients to add at the proper time.

- One can put one cup of the milk in the blender first.

- Then have another child add the Equal™ packets and ice.

- Next, one container of yogurt needs to be added, along with the frozen strawberries.

- The other container of yogurt needs to be added.

- Next, add frozen blueberries, and then top it off by pouring the other cup of milk over the top.

- Blend on "ice crush" setting until the frozen ingredients are broken up.

Then, continue to blend for a full minute.

It may be necessary to stop to stir if the mixture is not moving around the blender.

This will fill the blender.

Any leftovers can be kept in the refrigerator for 24 hours.

Whatcha Think?

What helps us grow strong? We need to exercise and get lots of sleep. But we also need to eat right.

Can you name some foods that are good for us to eat? We need to eat lots of fruits and vegetables. This snack is really good for you and will help you grow up, just like Jesus. (You may need to check that none of your kids are lactose intolerant.)

What did we put in our shake that is good for us? Would this be a good snack for you to have? God gave us good foods to help us grow.

COOKIE WELL

The Woman at the Well

John 4:1-42

The Goodies

1 package refrigerated chocolate cookie dough*

caramels

minimuffin pan

If chocolate cookie dough is not available, add 2 tablespoons of cocoa to sugar cookie dough and blend well.

Gadgets & Gizmos

cooking spray

plastic knife

napkin

The Main Thing

Even though the Jews despised the Samaritans, Jesus insisted that He and His disciples travel the road that led through Samaria. After traveling all day Jesus was tired. He sat down by a well and sent the disciples into town to get food. While He was sitting there, a woman came to draw water from the well. Immediately, she noticed that the man sitting at the well was a Jew, so she did not speak to Him. When she had drawn the water and was ready to leave, Jesus asked her for a drink. The woman wanted to know why a Jew was asking a Samaritan woman for water. Jesus told her that He could give her living water. "After drinking water from the well, you get thirsty again. But after drinking the living water of Jesus, you don't thirst again. Living water brings everlasting life." Jesus meant that living water was the salvation He brings. The woman listened closely as Jesus told her that He was the Messiah.

The Fun Stuff

Beforehand, preheat oven to 350°.

Lightly spray the minimuffin pan with cooking spray.

Give each child a piece of cookie dough, enough to make 1½ cookies.

Have kids press the cookie dough into the muffin pan so that it comes up the sides of the muffin cup completely. (You may need to chill before baking because of kids' handling.)

Say: *This is the well where the women met Jesus.*

Help the kids unwrap a caramel, cut it in half, and place both halves in the center of the cookie cup.

Bake according to the cookie dough package.

Say: *The caramel will melt and become the water in the well.*

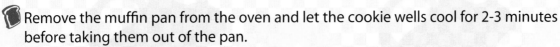 Remove the muffin pan from the oven and let the cookie wells cool for 2-3 minutes before taking them out of the pan.

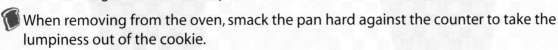 When removing from the oven, smack the pan hard against the counter to take the lumpiness out of the cookie.

Whatcha Think?

What did Jesus say that confused the woman?

How are the water from the well and living water different? How are they the same? It was very unusual for a Jew and a Samaritan to have a conversation, but the message Jesus has is for everyone!

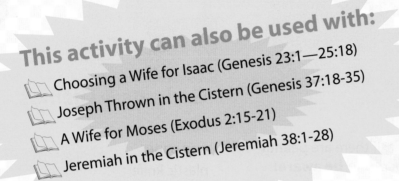

This activity can also be used with:

Choosing a Wife for Isaac (Genesis 23:1—25:18)

Joseph Thrown in the Cistern (Genesis 37:18-35)

A Wife for Moses (Exodus 2:15-21)

Jeremiah in the Cistern (Jeremiah 38:1-28)

PEANUT BUTTER DOUGH MAT

Jesus Heals the Lame Man

John 5:1-18

The Goodies

2 c creamy peanut butter
½ c honey
2 c powdered sugar

Special caution: If there are peanut allergies in your group, **be aware!**

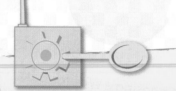

Gadgets & Gizmos

bowl
wax paper
plastic knife
plastic fork
craft stick

The Main Thing

Jesus came to the Pool of Bethesda where sick people gathered. They believed that when the waters of the pool moved, the first person in would be healed. Jesus asked the man if he wanted to be healed and the man said that he could never get in the water first because he always had to ask for help. Jesus told the man to pick up his mat and walk.

The religious leaders were upset with the man for carrying his mat, and they wanted to know who had healed him. But the man didn't know who Jesus was. Later, the man met Jesus at the temple. When he went to the religious leaders and told them who had healed him, the leaders were angry with Jesus for healing on the Sabbath. Jesus said He had healed the man because God was always at work and He was like His Father. This just made the religious leaders angrier.

The Fun Stuff

- Mix the peanut butter, honey and powdered sugar until it is play dough consistency.

- Instruct the children to flatten their peanut butter dough onto the wax paper and use the plastic knife to cut it into the largest rectangle possible out of the piece they have.

- Have kids use the fork to make fringe on the shorter ends by pressing down with the fork tines.

- Then have them press the edge of the craft stick into the peanut butter dough making parallel lines in both directions to make it look like it has been woven.

Whatcha Think?

- Have you ever sat on a mat? at the pool? at the beach?
- Why do people use a mat to sit on instead of sitting right on the ground?
- Why do you think Jesus told the man to pick up his mat? Why didn't Jesus just tell the man to walk?
- Why do you think the man forgot to ask who Jesus was?

HAPPY BIRD

God Will Take Care of You

Matthew 6:26-27

The Goodies

caramel popcorn
1 Twinkie™ snack cake
2 minichocolate chips
1 piece of candy corn
2 lemon jelly fruit slices
dab of canned icing

Gadgets & Gizmos

paper plate
plastic knife

The Main Thing

Jesus was teaching people—He had so many wonderful things to tell them! One thing Jesus taught as people gathered around Him was that they should not worry. He told them not to worry about their food or clothing or where they lived. To help them understand how God felt Jesus told them to think about the birds. Birds don't plant; they don't harvest or store up food in barns because they are afraid of what might happen tomorrow. That's because their Father in heaven takes care of them. Then Jesus comforted the people by telling them that they were much more valuable to God than birds. No amount of worrying will make you live one day longer!

The Fun Stuff

- Have kids cut the Twinkie™ in half and set it upright on the plate with the cut side against the plate. This is the bird's body.

- Let them push the 2 mini chocolate chips into the Twinkie™ for the eyes of the bird.

- Put a piece of candy corn into the Twinkie™ to make a beak.

- Put a dab of icing on one end of the smooth side of a lemon slice and stick it on the side of the Twinkie™ for a wing. One side of the lemon slice will be scalloped and the other edge will be smooth.

- Do the same on the other side for the other wing.

- Now, sprinkle caramel popcorn around the bottom of the Twinkie™ for the bird's nest.

Whatcha Think?

 What did Jesus tell the people to help them understand that they were valuable to God?

 What do birds eat for food?

 Where do they sleep? We're going to make a nice little nest for a bird to remind us that if God takes care of the birds, He will surely take care of us.

A COMMANDING TRAIL MIX

A Centurion's Servant Is Healed

Matthew 8:5-13, Luke 7:1-10

The Goodies

little granola clusters
raisins
Chex™ cereal
potato sticks
dried apricots

Gadgets & Gizmos

milk bottle cap
plastic knife
tablespoon
Styrofoam bowls
1/8 measuring cup
cookie jar
small plastic storage box

The Main Thing

A Roman centurion—someone who is in charge of 100 soldiers in the army—had a servant he loved who got very sick. The centurion had heard how Jesus healed people, so he asked the Jewish teachers in the synagogue to send for Jesus. They did just as the centurion had asked because this man had been very kind to them. As Jesus neared the centurion's house, he sent word to Jesus that he did not feel worthy to have Jesus come to his home, but he did know that Jesus had great power. As a centurion, the man had power over his soldiers and knew that he only had to tell them what to do and they would do it. The centurion believed that Jesus could just say the word and his servant would be well. Jesus was amazed at the man's faith and said that He had not seen such faith among the Jews. When another servant went to check on the sick servant, he found the man was healed!

The Fun Stuff

 Give each child a bowl and make the knife, tablespoon, milk bottle cap and measuring cup available.

Say: *In order to make your trail mix, you will have to follow my instructions exactly as I say.*

 One at a time give the following instructions to the children. Do not move to the next instruction until the previous one is completed.

Say: *Dip the milk bottle cap in the bowl of raisins. Dump the raisins from the bottle cap into your trail mix bowl.*

Go to the cabinet to find some Chex™ cereal. Count out 12 pieces of Chex™ cereal and put them in your trail mix bowl.

Go to the cookie jar. Inside the jar are potato sticks. Fill the measuring cup with the sticks and put them in your trail mix bowl.

Find the small plastic storage box. Get a spoonful of the granola clusters out of the box and put it in your trail mix bowl.

Take one dried apricot from the plate on the table and cut it into 8 pieces with the plastic knife.

Put the apricot pieces in the trail mix bowl.

Whatcha Think?

When I told you what to do to make the trail mix, you did it.

Why did you follow my instructions?

Why was the centurion sure that Jesus could make his servant well even when He wasn't there?

What could the centurion do in his job?

Why do people follow orders from someone else?

Now, have the children feed each other the trail mix. If there is one element of the trail mix they do not like, they must trust their partner not to feed that to them.

How did the centurion trust Jesus?

What did Jesus say about the faith of the centurion?

BREAD DOUGH PIGS

Jesus Heals a Wild Man

Matthew 8:28-34; Mark 5:1-20; Luke 8:26-39

The Goodies

2 frozen dinner roll doughs, thawed
cooking spray

Gadgets & Gizmos

craft paintbrush
aluminum foil
cookie sheet
plastic knife

The Main Thing

A wild man lived in a cemetery. He wandered around, crying and doing terrible things to himself. The demons of Satan were torturing him. When the wild man saw Jesus, the demons within him yelled at Jesus. Jesus called to the demon and asked its name. The answer came back that the name was Legion, meaning *many*, because there were actually many demons living in the man. The demons begged Jesus to send them into a herd of 2,000 pigs that were nearby, and Jesus said, "Go!" When the demons entered the pigs the animals took off running down the mountainside and into the sea where they drowned. News spread quickly to a nearby town and people came to see what happened. They were amazed, but so frightened by Jesus' power they asked Him to leave. The healed man followed Jesus and the disciples, but Jesus told him to go home and tell people about the miracle God had given him.

The Fun Stuff

- Give each child a piece of aluminum foil and the dough for two thawed dinner rolls.
- Spray the foil lightly with cooking spray.
- Press down one roll into a flat circle.
- Use the other roll for the features of the pig.
- Flatten the dinner roll.
- Cut a circle out of it about the size of a quarter. Place this in the center of the full roll you have flattened into a circle—this will be the pig's nose.
- To make the pig's nostrils, push the end of a craft paintbrush as far as it will go into the dough to make two holes.
- Cut two long triangles from the remainder of the dough. Attach them for ears at the top of the pig's head.

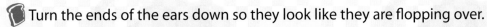

Turn the ends of the ears down so they look like they are flopping over.

Bake at package recommendation, watching for the dough to turn a golden brown.

Whatcha Think?

When Jesus chased the demons out of the man, where did He send them?

Why do you think Jesus chose to send the demons into the pigs?

Why do you think it took 2,000 pigs to hold the demons?

Would this have scared you if you had seen it?

Why do you think the people asked Jesus to leave their town?

The activity can also be used with:

The Prodigal Son
(Luke 15:11-32)

GRAHAM CRACKER MAT

Through the Roof

Matthew 9:2-8; Mark 2:1-12; Luke 5:18-26

The Goodies

full graham cracker
canned white icing
E.L. Fudge™ cookie

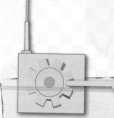

Gadgets & Gizmos

custard cup
paper plate
plastic knife (or craft stick)

The Main Thing

Jesus was staying at a certain house and the people of the town found out He was there. They started coming to listen to Him and to be healed. Soon, the house was wall-to-wall people. There was a crippled man whose four friends wanted desperately for Jesus to heal him. They carried the man to the house where Jesus was, but they couldn't get inside because of the crowd. They had an idea and carried the crippled man on his cot to the roof of the house. There, the friends dug a hole in the roof of the house big enough for the man and his cot to fit through. People in the house were astonished to see four men lowering a crippled man through a hole in the ceiling, right in front of Jesus. Jesus told the man his sins were forgiven, then told him to get up, pick up his mat and go home. The faith of the man's friends had touched Jesus' heart. The man joined his friends and they left that house with much joy.

The Fun Stuff

- Beforehand, put manageable amounts of icing in small heavy containers, like glass custard cups, that won't tip over with the weight of a plastic knife.

- Let the children ice one side of the graham cracker.

  Ask: *What was the man lying on? The graham cracker is the cot and the icing is a blanket. Why was the man lying on the cot?*

- Place the E.L. Fudge™ cookie on the mat so the crippled man is lying down.

Whatcha Think?

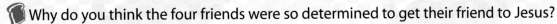 Why do you think the four friends were so determined to get their friend to Jesus?

 How do you think the four friends made the crippled man feel?

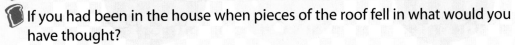 If you had been in the house when pieces of the roof fell in what would you have thought?

ROUGH JELL-O™ SEA

Jesus Walks on Water

Matthew 14:23-36; Mark 6:47-56; John 6:16-29

The Goodies

blue Jell-O™

"people" cracker or cookie (E.L. Fudge™)

Gadgets & Gizmos

fork

clear cup

The Main Thing

After a long day of teaching the people, Jesus decided to go up the mountain to pray while the disciples got in a boat. During the night a storm came. The boat was tossed about by huge waves and strong winds. The disciples wished Jesus was with them because they had seen Him calm a storm before. Jesus knew the disciples would be frightened by the storm, so He came down from the mountain and started walking across the sea…on top of the water!

Through the mist and fog the disciples saw someone coming toward them. At first they thought it was a ghost, but then they heard Jesus' voice. Peter called out to Jesus that if it was really Him, then Jesus should call for Peter to walk on the water also. Jesus did just that. Peter was walking on the water when he looked around and saw the big waves. Immediately, he started to sink, but Jesus reached out to save him. When they got into the boat the disciples worshiped Jesus.

The Fun Stuff

- Give each child a serving of blue Jell-O™ in a clear cup.
- Let them use a fork to stir up the Jell-O™ to make a turbulent sea.
- Place a "people" cookie or cracker on top of the stormy sea and pretend it is walking across the water.

Whatcha Think?

- During the storm the sea was very rough. Does this Jell-O™ look like a calm sea or a stormy sea?

When the disciples were in the middle of the storm, what do you think they thought was going to happen to them?

 How do you think the other disciples felt when they saw Peter walking on the water?

BAA-BAA SNACK

Parable of the Lost Sheep

Matthew 18:12-14; Luke 15:3-7

The Goodies

1" slice of pound cake
vanilla wafer
pink and black jelly beans
can of whipped white icing

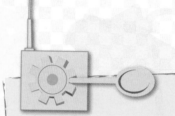

Gadgets & Gizmos

craft stick
3" diameter circle cookie cutter
(or use the rim of a glass)
paper plate

The Main Thing

Jesus was trying to help the people understand what God is like. Many times He did that by using special stories that had a heavenly meaning. The Pharisees noticed that Jesus was eating with people who were known to sin. So Jesus told the Pharisees this story: There was a shepherd who had 100 sheep. One of them was missing, so he left the 99 and went looking for the lost one. He searched and searched until he found it. He cleaned the sheep and carried it home, celebrating that he had found the one that was lost. Jesus told them all heaven celebrates in the same way when one sinner turns to God.

The Fun Stuff

- Beforehand, cut vanilla wafers in half.
- Place a slice of pound cake (big enough that the cookie cutter will be able to fit in it) on a paper plate.
- Have children use a cookie cutter to cut a circle. The remainder around the edge can be set aside to eat as they work.
- Let children ice the round piece of cake, including the edges.
- Have them stand two pink jellybeans on end and push into the cake for eyes.
- Do the same with a black jellybean for the nose.
- Spread icing on the two half vanilla wafers and add as the sheep's ears.

Whatcha Think?

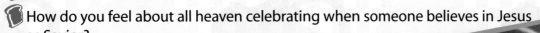 Why did Jesus tell parables (stories)?

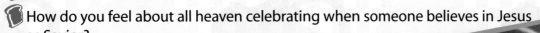 Why did Jesus tell the parable about the sheep that was lost?

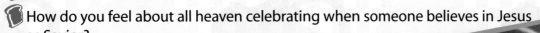 How do you think the shepherd felt when he had to leave the 99 sheep behind?

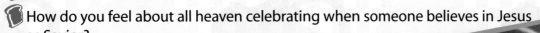 Where do you think the lost sheep was?

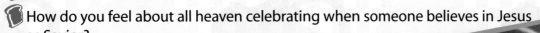 How did the shepherd feel when he found the lost sheep?

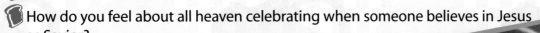 How do you feel about all heaven celebrating when someone believes in Jesus as Savior?

FORGIVENESS CRUMBS

How Many Times Should We Forgive?

Matthew 18:21-35

The Goodies

chocolate mini-sandwich cookies

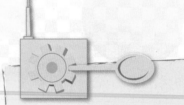

Gadgets & Gizmos

Zip-lock sandwich bag
spoon
rolling pin (or 6" piece of 1" dowel rod)

The Main Thing

One time Peter asked Jesus how many times he was expected to forgive someone who had wronged him. He wanted to know if seven times was enough. Jesus told him that he needed to forgive not seven times, but seven times seventy. In other words, he shouldn't try to count how many times and he should always be willing to forgive. God is always willing to forgive us and we should be willing to forgive others.

The Fun Stuff

🍞 Have kids count out 7 chocolate mini-sandwich cookies and place them in their Zip-lock bag as they respond to:

Ask: *Are we supposed to forgive once? Twice? Three times (and so on)? How many times did Jesus tell Peter that he should forgive?*

🍞 Make sure the bag is fastened completely.

Ask: *Is forgiving someone seven times enough?*

🍞 Let the children use the rolling pin to crush the cookies. Tell them, "Be careful not to pound on them, because the bag will tear if you attempt to do this too roughly. Now, look at the number of pieces that are in the bag."

Whatcha Think?

 Does anyone want to count the number of pieces of cookie you have in your bag? Why not? There are so many it would be difficult to count them. Let's continue to forgive people, even if it's so many times we can't count them.

APPLE FACE

Little Children Are Brought to Jesus

Matthew 19:13-15; Mark 10:13-16

The Goodies

apple

assortment of little candies (*gumdrops, candy corn, Dots™, jelly fruit slices*)

assortment of small pieces of fruit (*pineapple, small grapes, kiwi slices, banana slices*)

black and red Twizzlers™

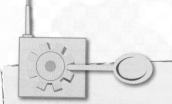

Gadgets & Gizmos

plastic knife
paper plate
construction paper
scissors
toothpicks

The Main Thing

A large crowd was surrounding Jesus as He spoke God's truth. Some mothers brought their children, hoping they could get close to Jesus, but the people were pressed against one another. When they did manage to get close, the disciples ushered them away, saying that Jesus was too busy and couldn't be bothered with the children. Jesus heard what was happening and stopped the disciples from sending the children away. As Jesus pulled the children close to Him, He told the disciples that the kingdom of God is made up of those who are like children and unless people become like a child, they will never enter the kingdom of God. Jesus knew how innocent the children were and how eager they were to draw close to God.

The Fun Stuff

Say: *The children who were brought to Jesus were all different, just like all of you are different. Let's celebrate how we're all different and yet Jesus loves each child!*

- Set out an assortment of small candies and fruit pieces.
- Make available small pieces of construction paper and scissors.
- Let the children use the apples for their head.
- Break the toothpicks in half for the kids to stick fruit and candy features into the apple.
- Use pieces of fruit and candy as much as possible, but the construction paper is available if needed.
- If pieces of fruit need to be cut in different sizes or shapes, kids can use the plastic knife to tailor it for the apple.
- Remind them about those little features like eyebrows.

COOKIE CRUMB SAND

The Sinful Woman Brought to Jesus

John 8:1-11

The Goodies

2 light sandwich cookies

Gadgets & Gizmos

heavy Zip-lock sandwich bags
paper plate
dowel rod rolling pins (1" x 6" long)
plastic spoon

The Main Thing

The Pharisees were always trying to catch Jesus doing or saying something wrong. One day they brought a woman to Jesus and told Him they had caught her doing something that was sinful. According to the law they had the right to throw stones at her. The Pharisees asked Jesus what they should do. Jesus knew they were trying to trick Him, so He didn't say anything. He just stooped down and began writing something in the sand. The men got angry and asked again. Still, Jesus kept writing in the sand. Then He looked up at them and said, "Whoever has never sinned should be the first one to throw a stone." As they thought about their own sins, one by one they left. When they were all gone Jesus looked up at the woman and asked her where the men were that accused her. She said they had gone. Jesus told her to go also, but not to sin anymore.

The Fun Stuff

Have children place 2 vanilla (or other light) sandwich cookies in a Zip-lock sandwich bag, push the air out and close it tightly.

Check the bags to make sure they are sealed tightly before allowing the children to move on.

Use the dowel rod rolling pin to crush the sandwich cookies. (Too much air in the bag makes this difficult.)

Keep crushing until the crumbs are very fine and look like sand.

Pour the crumbs out of the bag onto a paper plate.

Use your finger to write your initials in the cookie crumb sand.

Whatcha Think?

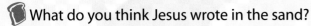 What do you think Jesus wrote in the sand?

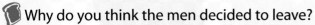 Why do you think the men decided to leave?

 Do you think the woman was happy? Write your answer in your cookie crumb sand.

Let the children scrape their crumbs into a pile on their plate and eat them with a spoon.

PUDDING IN A BAG

Jesus Heals the Man Born Blind

John 9

The Goodies

2 T chocolate pudding mix

½ c milk (not skim)

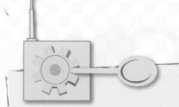

Gadgets & Gizmos

heavy sandwich or quart Zip-lock bags

covering for table

tablespoons

plastic spoons

The Main Thing

As Jesus left the temple on the Sabbath He saw a man who had been born blind sitting alongside the road. When the disciples asked who had sinned to cause the man to be blind, Jesus replied that he was blind so that God's power could be shown. Jesus spit into the dust and made mud. He smeared the mud on the blind man's eyes and told him to go wash it off in the pool of Siloam. As soon as the mud was washed off of the man's eyes, he could see again. Those who saw the miracle had many questions, but the man who was healed believed that Jesus must be the Son of God to have the power to do such wonderful things.

The Fun Stuff

- Beforehand, cover the table with a plastic cloth, just in case a bag doesn't stay closed.

- Place all the chocolate pudding mix in one bowl.

- Let the children measure out two tablespoons of the pudding powder and put it in their Zip-lock bag.

  Ask: *How did Jesus make the mud? We have our "dust" pudding powder, but we need to make it into mud. Let's add some milk.*

- Have each child hold the bag open while an adult pours ½ c milk into it.

- Immediately, the adult will secure the Zip-lock bag, trying to push some of the air out in the process.

- Have the kids lay the bag on the table and start gently massaging the bag to mix the ingredients. This will take several minutes.

- When the mixture has the consistency of pudding, the bag can be opened and the pudding eaten with a spoon.

Whatcha Think?

🍞 Mud seems like a very strange thing to use to heal someone. We shouldn't be surprised by Jesus' power!

🍞 The man who had been healed was getting irritated with all the questions he was being asked. Why do you think he was getting irritated?

🍞 What helped the blind man believe that Jesus was the Son of God?

This snack activity could also be used with:

📖 The Prodigal Son
(Luke 15:11-32)

GRAVE CLOTHES

Come Forth, Lazarus!

John 11:1-44

The Goodies

Lit'L Smokie™ wieners
filo dough

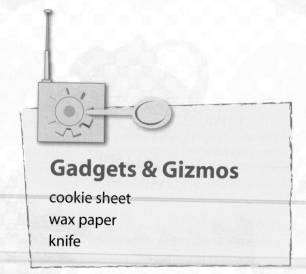

Gadgets & Gizmos

cookie sheet
wax paper
knife

The Main Thing

Lazarus and his two sisters, Mary and Martha, were very good friends of Jesus. Lazarus got sick and his sisters sent for Jesus to come. Jesus delayed going to Lazarus and when He did arrive, Lazarus was already dead and buried. The sisters wondered why Jesus had not come right away because they knew Jesus could have healed their brother.

Jesus asked to be taken to the tomb. As He approached the grave, He cried at his friend's loss. Jesus asked that the stone covering the opening to the grave be moved and Martha tried to stop Him. She pointed out that Lazarus had been dead long enough that there would be a terrible smell. When the stone was moved, Jesus cried out in a loud voice, "Lazarus, come forth!" In a moment, Lazarus appeared at the entrance to the tomb and the people were astonished. They rushed to him to remove the grave clothes and marveled that Jesus was able to raise someone from the dead.

The Fun Stuff

- Filo dough can be found in the frozen food section near the pastries. It is very thin, flakey dough that dries out quickly if not covered with a damp cloth.

- Thaw the dough slowly. When it's time to make the snack, open the dough package and cut several sheets at a time into ½" strips.

- Give each child one section of strips that have been cut. Place it on a piece of wax paper he or she can use as a work place.

- Have the kids wrap the filo dough strips around a smokey link, criss-crossing the dough as it goes around. They can use as many strips as necessary to completely cover the link with about 10 layers of filo dough.

- Place the wrapped link on a cookie sheet.

- Bake in a preheated oven at 350° for 10-12 minutes until golden brown.

Whatcha Think?

- What does this snack remind you of?

- Who was wrapped in grave clothes? This snack reminds us of Lazarus when he was dead and wrapped in the grave clothes.

- What did Jesus say when the stone was rolled away from the tomb?

- What did the people do when they saw Lazarus? They rushed to him and took the grave clothes off of him.

ROLL THE COOKIE AWAY

The Empty Tomb

Matthew 28:1-7, Mark 16:1-7, Luke 24:1-7, John 20:1

The Goodies

spice cupcake with creamy filling
chocolate sandwich cookie

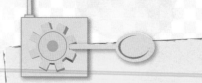

Gadgets & Gizmos

plastic knife
paper plate

The Main Thing

Jesus had been laid in the grave. At dawn the earth began to tremble and an angel came to roll away the stone that covered the opening to the tomb. The soldiers guarding the tomb were terrified by what they saw and fled. Some women came to the garden and found the stone rolled away from the tomb. They saw an angel in the tomb who told them that Jesus was not there; He had risen. Then they ran to tell the other followers.

The Fun Stuff

- Place the spice cupcake on the plate.
- Using the plastic knife, slice a piece down the side to expose the filling within.
- Place the chocolate sandwich cookie next to the exposed cupcake where it can be rolled in front of the tomb's entrance, or can be rolled away.
- As the children roll the cookie away, they should say, "He is not here. He is risen!"

Whatcha Think?

- How do you think the women felt as they were walking to the tomb?
- How do you think they felt when they saw the angel?
- How do you think they felt after they heard the angel's words and saw the empty tomb where Jesus had been?

YUMMY PANCAKES

Breakfast on the Shore

John 21:1-23

The Goodies

pancake mix

milk or water

¼ c measuring cup

spray cooking oil

syrup

toppings for pancakes

Gadgets & Gizmos

large cup

spoon

spatula

paper plates

griddle

(Depending on the size of the group, you may need more than one griddle.)

The Main Thing

After Jesus rose from the tomb, but before He went back to heaven, He appeared to the disciples several times. One of those times was when the disciples had been fishing all night. Jesus was on the shore where He built a fire. When the disciples came in to shore, Jesus made breakfast for them from the fish they caught. We don't eat fish for breakfast (or do you?), but we do eat pancakes. So, let's celebrate Jesus being with His disciples on the shore for breakfast by eating our pancakes!

The Fun Stuff

- Let the children put ¼ c of pancake mix in their cup.

- Then have them add ¼ c of liquid to that and stir. (This is based on Hungry Jack pancake mix.)

- Make sure the preheated, hot griddle is supervised by an adult.

- Lightly spray cooking oil on the griddle.

- Allow the kids to pour their pancake mix onto the griddle. Their individual amount should make one large pancake.

- With supervision the children should be able to flip their own pancake and take it from the griddle to a paper plate.

- They will then finish their pancake with the toppings you have provided.

Whatcha Think?

- How do you think the disciples felt when they saw Jesus on the shore?
- What did Jesus use to make breakfast?
- Why do you think Jesus made breakfast for the disciples?
- What do you think was the most important part of the breakfast?

Fish sprinkles to add to the pancakes can be purchased online from www.sugarcraft.com.

This activity can also be used with:

The Widow Feeds Elijah
(1 Kings 17:10-24)

A RECIPE IN CODE

Philip and the Ethiopian

Acts 8:26-40

The Goodies

1 spoonful sharp cheese spread

1 spoonful soft cream cheese

shake of Worchestershire sauce

pinch of garlic powder

pinch of onion powder

celery

crackers

pretzels

Gadgets & Gizmos

cup

spoon

The Main Thing

The Lord told Philip to walk along a certain road. A royal chariot from Ethiopia was going down the road also, carrying a man reading a Bible scroll. His face was sad as he read because he didn't understand. The Lord told Philip to run up to the chariot and ask the Ethiopian if he understood what he was reading. The man said, "How can I understand when I have no one to teach me what it means?" So, Philip rode along with the man and explained the scriptures to him. The Ethiopian became a believer in Jesus Christ. They stopped the chariot by some water and Philip baptized the man as a believer.

The Fun Stuff

- Copy the recipe on the next page and place one on each child's seat.
- Place the ingredients in the center of the table and give each child a cup and a spoon.
- Tell the children to follow the recipe to make a really good snack.
- They will question how to follow the crazy recipe. It seems to be in code.

Whatcha Think?

- What kind of help do you need to make this recipe?
- Who do you think can help you?
- Why do you think I can help you? You need help understanding what the recipe really says and I am the one who can help you understand. The Ethiopian didn't understand the Bible scroll until Philip came along. Philip knew what the words meant and was willing to share with the Ethiopian.

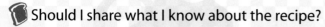 Should I share what I know about the recipe?

    Reveal what the symbols mean for each of the ingredients:

      1 <u>spoonful</u> of <u>sharp cheddar cheese spread</u>

      1 <u>spoonful</u> of <u>soft creamed cheese</u>

      1 <u>shake</u> of <u>Worchestershire sauce</u>

      1 <u>pinch</u> of <u>garlic powder</u>

      1 <u>pinch</u> of <u>onion powder</u>

Reveal them one at a time and encourage the children to make guesses as to what they are.

They will be able to figure out some of the amounts that repeat by what is left on the table that hasn't been used.

As each ingredient and amount is revealed, the children will add that to their cup.

When all the ingredients are in the cup, stir to combine the ingredients thoroughly.

Now, put some on a cracker, pretzel or piece of celery and enjoy a really good snack.

A GOOD SNACK

Mix:

UNUSUAL EYES

Saul on the Road to Damascus

Acts 9:1-19

The Goodies

roll of sugar cookie dough

canned cream cheese icing

kiwi

banana

grapes

Twizzlers™

Gadgets & Gizmos

paper plate

craft stick

The Main Thing

Saul hated those who believed in Jesus as the Son of God, so much so that he spent his time hunting them down and punishing them severely. He was on his way to Damascus to arrest the Christians there when a bright light came down on Saul. He fell to the ground and heard a voice say, "Saul, why are you persecuting me?" When Saul asked who was speaking to him, the voice said that it was Jesus. Jesus told Saul to go into the city and find a certain house and stay there. As Saul got up from the ground he realized he could not see; he was blind!

The men with him took him to the house where Saul waited for three days. Then God sent Ananias to Saul. When Ananias laid his hands on Saul his eyes were healed and he could see again. That was a miracle, but the miracle that was even more wonderful was that Saul became a believer in Jesus Christ himself.

The Fun Stuff

Beforehand, prepare the sugar cookies as instructed on the package, making them a little smaller than normal.

Each child will use two sugar cookies.

Have them spread a thin coating of icing over the cookies.

Have them create a pair of eyes by layering slices of kiwi, banana, and then making the pupils from half a grape.

Use Twizzlers™ to make a smile.

Whatcha Think?

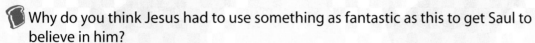 Why do you think Jesus had to use something as fantastic as this to get Saul to believe in him?

How do you think Saul felt during the three days he had to wait?

How do you think Ananias felt when God told him to go to Saul?

Why would Ananias be frightened?

A CRUNCHY FIRE

Shipwrecked but Safe

Acts 28:1-10

The Goodies

1/3 c crispy chow mein noodles

gummy worm

1 c peanut butter or butterscotch chips

1 t shortening

1/3 measuring cup

Special caution: If there are peanut allergies in your group, be sure those children use the butterscotch chips.

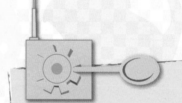

Gadgets & Gizmos

microwaveable bowl

plastic spoon

small piece of wax paper

wooden spoon

The Main Thing

Paul was a prisoner because he had preached about Jesus. He was being taken to Rome by ship to stand trial before Caesar when a violent storm came and the ship fell apart. All the men on board swam to a nearby island. Paul started a fire by placing sticks in a pile. The movement disturbed a snake that was hidden in the sticks. It came out of the fire and bit Paul on the hand. The people from the island watched Paul because they knew the snake that had bitten him was poisonous. God protected Paul and nothing happened to him. The islanders were amazed and thought that Paul was a god. But Paul took the opportunity to tell them about Jesus. Many believed during the three months that Paul and the others were stranded there.

The Fun Stuff

- Have each child measure and pour 1/3 c of chow mein noodles into his or her Styrofoam bowl.
- Place the peanut butter chips and the shortening in a microwaveable bowl.
- Start melting the chips by placing them in the microwave on high for about a minute.
- Stir, then continue to melt by placing in the microwave for 20 seconds at a time, stirring between each 20-second interval.
- While the melted chips are still warm, dish out a spoonful onto the top of the chow mein noodles.

Have children stir their noodles and peanut butter until the noodles are completely covered.

Say: *When the men made it to the island after the ship broke apart, what did they do?*

Move the mixture onto the wax paper where they can form it to look like a bonfire.

Say: *What came out of the fire and threatened Paul's safety?*

Place a gummy worm coming out of the fire.

Whatcha Think?

What do you suppose the islanders thought was going to happen to Paul?

What did the islanders do when they saw that the snake's bite did not affect Paul?

How did Paul use this opportunity for God? Even though Paul was a prisoner because he taught about Jesus, he kept talking about Him to whoever would listen.

CANDLESTICK

Light of the World

John 8:12, John 3:19-21, Ephesians 5:8, Psalm 119:105

The Goodies

pineapple ring

½ stick of string cheese

candy corn

½ marshmallow

Gadgets & Gizmos

paper plate

The Main Thing

Use this snack idea to help in a discussion of any of these "light" scriptures.

Psalm 119:105 - Your Word is a lamp to my feet and a light for my path.

John 8:12 - I am the light of the world. Whoever follows me will never walk in darkness, but will have the light of life.

John 3:19-21 - Light has come into the world, but men loved darkness instead of light because their deeds were evil. Everyone who does evil hates the light, and will not come into the light for fear that his deeds will be exposed. But whoever lives by the truth comes into the light, so that it may be seen plainly that what he has done has been done through God.

Ephesians 5:8 - For you were once darkness, but now you are light in the Lord. Live as children of light.

The Fun Stuff

Lay a pineapple ring on a paper plate.

Stuff half a marshmallow in the hole of the pineapple.

Push the half-stick of string cheese into the marshmallow. This will make a candle.

Push the wide end of a piece of candy corn into the top of the string cheese to make the candle flame.

Read John 3:19-21. Every time the word "light" is used, replace it with "the presence of God." This will help the children understand the symbolism of light in this verse.

Whatcha Think?

- Name some things that give light.
- Why is light important?
- When have you wished there was more light?

FUN WITH COOKIE CUTTERS

This book is full of fun ways to make edible snacks that reinforce Bible stories and initiate conversation. None of the ideas, though, include the use of cookie cutters, which are always fun utensils to use with children.

Consider cutting out something other than cookie dough when you pull out the cookie cutters. Try creating interest with your children by using a cookie cutter with:

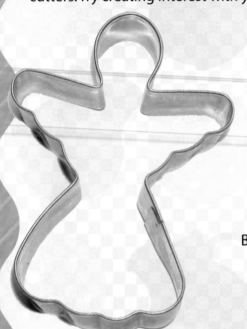

Sandwiches

Grilled cheese

Specialty breads

Pancakes

Cheese slices

Jell-O™

Pound cake

Brownies

Bologna or other lunch meat

Tortillas

Hamburgers

Meatloaf

Some cookie cutter shapes you might want to consider using are:

Pig (Prodigal son)

Heart (Salvation lessons)

Angel (Anytime an angel appears)

Star (Wise men)

Animals (Noah)

Person

Hand (Serving)

Foot (Following Jesus)

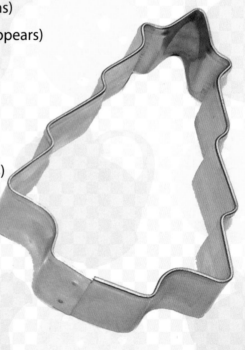

Store-bought packaged sugar cookie dough works well with cookie cutters, if it is rolled out onto a lightly floured surface. If you would rather make the dough yourself (saves money), then here's a great recipe to use.

2 c flour

1 c sugar

½ t salt

1 t baking powder

1 c shortening

1 egg

1 t vanilla

1 T water

Mix together in a small bowl the egg, vanilla, and water.

Sift together the salt, baking powder, flour, and sugar.

Blend the shortening into the dry ingredients. Add the egg, vanilla, and water and continue to blend until the dough is thoroughly mixed and smooth. Form the dough into a ball. Roll onto a floured board and cut the cookies. Place on an ungreased cookie sheet and bake at 375° for 6-8 minutes.

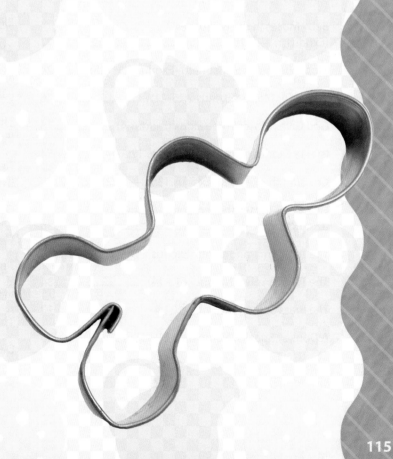

STORY INDEX

Old Testament

New Testament

SCRIPTURE INDEX

Old Testament

New Testament

NOTES